Ready Steady Baby!

A guide to pregnancy,
birth and early parenthood

Acknowledgements

This book reflects many discussions, suggestions and comments made by health professionals, professional bodies, lay and voluntary organisations, and parents. The Health Education Board for Scotland (HEBS) would like to thank all of those who contributed in any way to the development of this project, for so willingly giving their time, and sharing their expertise and experience.

Special thanks to the task group responsible for working on this project, especially Gill Allan, Linda Bryce, Sally Callaghan, Nadine Edwards, Kirsty Foster, Agnes McGowan, Jean Muir and Riny Wondergem.
Dr Sheila Lawson, Dr Angus Ford and Clare Keenan also provided valuable input and support.

Particular thanks to all the parents who gave permission for us to take and use photographs of themselves and their children.

This book was produced with the support of Borders Community Health Services NHS Trust, Dundee Teaching Hospital (Ninewells), Lanarkshire Health Board, Law Hospital NHS Trust, Lothian Health and West Lothian NHS Trust.

Original text: Heather Welford

Design: Design Links, Edinburgh

Photography: Iain Stewart. Page 78 Collections/Anthea Sieveking—thanks to Janet Balaskas and the Active Birth Movement for their part in arranging these pictures.

Published by the Health Education Board for Scotland, Woodburn House, Canaan Lane, Edinburgh EH10 4SG

© Health Education Board for Scotland 1998

First published 1998

ISBN   1-902030-02-8

Repro by Interface
Printed in Great Britain by MacDonald Lindsay Pindar PLC

Every effort has been made to ensure that this publication is as up to date and accurate as possible. However, new medical research can sometimes mean that information about pregnancy and childbirth, and recommendations for childcare change very quickly. Changes and alterations will be made at the next reprint to reflect any new information, and significant changes in recommendations will be made at once to doctors, midwives and health visitors.

While the book represents the consensus of good practice, please remember that different circumstances and clinical judgement may mean that you have slightly different patterns of care.

If you have any doubts, worries or fears, then do not hesitate to contact your doctor, midwife or health visitor for reassurance and further explanations.

Contents

About this book

Welcome to *Ready Steady Baby!* We have produced this book to give clear and up-to-date information about pregnancy, childbirth and caring for your child up to the age of three. We hope that you will enjoy reading it, and will keep it to refer to in the future.

If you want to look up a specific topic, there is an index at the back of the book.

Written by an experienced author who is also a mother herself, along with a team of experts, we hope that it will answer your questions, and lessen any concerns that you may have.

Remember that there are many people who will be caring for you and your baby—if you need to talk to anyone in more detail about any aspect of your care, or your baby's health or development, then please don't hesitate to contact your doctor, midwife or health visitor.

Early pregnancy

THE FIRST SIGNS

If you have a regular menstrual cycle, you may notice you miss a period about two weeks after you conceived. You may have other signs as well — you may even be aware of some of them before you notice your missed period, especially if you're hoping to be pregnant, and watching for changes. Arrange a visit to your GP to have your pregnancy confirmed and discuss antenatal care.

Changes within your body occur because of pregnancy hormones, which are released into your bloodstream, and which affect various parts of your body.

- **Your breasts start to change soon after you conceive.** Your body starts to make tissue for producing and storing milk. You may feel your breasts are more tender than usual. Tiny spots around the nipple area — called tubercles — become more obvious.

- **You may feel sick, and go off certain foods and smells.** Some women do vomit. This usually happens in the mornings, but it can happen at other times as well. A metallic taste in your mouth may affect your sense of taste. The smell of some foods may make you feel unwell.

- **You may feel tired.** Some women say they feel more tired in early pregnancy than at any other time.

- **You may need to pass urine more often.**

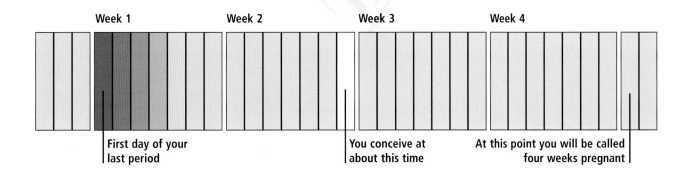

Week 1   Week 2   Week 3   Week 4

First day of your
last period

You conceive at
about this time

At this point you will be called
four weeks pregnant

'I always had an idea I'd
be a mum some day, but
now it's going to happen,
I don't really know what
my feelings are. It's come as
a shock. I told my boyfriend
and he was so pleased.
I know he expected me to
feel the same. But I can't.
I'm hoping I will change
— it's early days yet.'

'I'm so excited, I can't
wait to tell everyone —
I'm looking forward to
having a bump so I can
look pregnant as well as
feel it!'

'I have felt so ill these last
three weeks — sick not just
in the mornings but in the
afternoons and evenings as
well — and tired, too.
Feeling this bad takes the
edge off feeling good
about the pregnancy.'

questions answered

Q. When is your baby due?

**A. Pregnancy usually lasts 40 weeks, or between nine
and nine-and-a-half calendar months. This is based
on the average length of a menstrual cycle, which
is 28 days. The start of your pregnancy is dated
from the first day of your last period, even though
you conceived after this. If you usually have your
period more often, or less often, than every 28
days, the date you expect your baby should take
that into account.**

● It's helpful to think of the 'due date' as only a
rough guide. Very few women (around five per
cent) actually give birth on the date they are
'due'. Most babies come at some time during the
fortnight before or the fortnight after this date.

● If you don't know when your last period was,
your midwife or doctor can use other signs
and symptoms to establish the length of your
pregnancy. You may also be offered an
ultrasound scan.

YOUR IDENTITY AS 'YOU'

Sometimes, you may feel your own identity is lost — the focus is on you as a mother, and not you as a person who has lots of other aspects to her life besides this. But on the whole, the attention you get in pregnancy is warm, and well worth enjoying.

It's usual to have some anxieties about your health or the development of your baby. You'll be thinking ahead to the birth, too. If something is troubling you, you can talk to your midwife about it in confidence. If you don't yet have a telephone number for a midwife, contact your hospital, family doctor or health centre and ask to be put in touch with a midwife.

'People relate to you differently when you're pregnant. I feel my friends are looking forward to the baby, too — everyone's so interested.'

'I feel I've got closer to my mother since becoming pregnant — she's started to share memories of her own pregnancies with me, and we've had some good long chats together.'

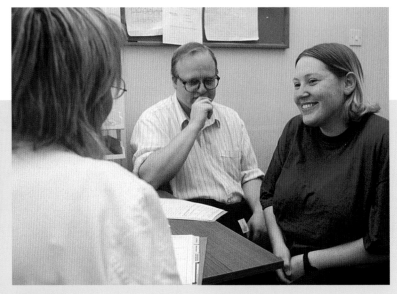

BEING INVOLVED

FATHERS share many of the same feelings as mothers during pregnancy. If you're a father-to-be, you may sometimes be anxious and nervous about your baby's health and your partner's health. You may be delighted, but also wonder what the labour and birth will be like, and how you will cope. Here are some fathers' experiences.

'I found it hard going. Liz was very emotional and touchy in the first few months, partly because we lost a baby two years ago, and she was worried it would happen again. It was quite difficult. Towards the end, things got easier from that aspect, but she had high blood pressure and was told to rest. She needed a lot of support and encouragement.'

'I feel good about being a father — I really do. I love the fact that Yvonne is pregnant, and the way her body is changing. I actually feel proud of her, and of me. There have been times when I have started to think ahead, and I get a bit worried about the changes it will bring, but I think we'll cope. The positives outweigh the negatives.'

Fitness & health in pregnancy

What you do, and how you live your life, affects your baby. Making changes can make a difference.
A lot of the advice and information in this book will answer many of your questions and help you to care for your health at this important time.

SMOKING

You probably know that smoking can affect your baby now and in the future:

- smoking raises the levels of carbon monoxide in your blood, and less oxygen will reach your baby

- harmful chemicals reach your baby

- nicotine constricts the blood vessels on your side of the placenta, which means oxygen is passed over less efficiently to the baby.

The result is that the baby grows less well and will be born lighter. Low birth weight may mean problems during and after labour, and the baby may pick up infections more easily. Smoking also affects brain development and the general health of your baby. The effects have been shown to last into childhood, and beyond. There is also evidence that partners who smoke affect the baby's health — whether or not the pregnant woman smokes herself.

If you stop smoking, your baby is:

- less likely to be born before she or he is ready

- less likely to have breathing problems

- better able to resist infection

- less at risk from cot death, infection and chronic conditions such as asthma.

If you or your partner stop smoking you reduce all of these risks. Toddlers and children grow up healthier in a smoke-free atmosphere.

Stop smoking!

Giving up is worthwhile at any time in pregnancy — the sooner the better. Help yourself by:

- giving up with your partner, or a friend
- putting aside the money you have saved, and spending it on a treat
- taking up something you can't do at the same time as smoking — sewing, knitting, or another craft.

It is important to stay stopped once your baby has been born.

'I stopped just like that. A case of mind over matter. Had two girls and needed cash for other things. They don't smoke and neither do I.'

Ex-smoker with support from Smokeline

ALCOHOL

Some women don't like the taste of alcohol when they're pregnant, so they stop drinking it. If you don't stop, alcohol does reach your baby, but the evidence is that light, occasional drinking — one or two units, once or twice a week — is not likely to do any harm. Heavy drinking is associated with miscarriage, and sometimes with serious effects on your baby's development.

1 UNIT=

¹/₂ pint ordinary strength beer, lager or cider

OR

a single measure of spirit (whisky, gin, bacardi, vodka, etc)

OR

a small glass of wine

OR

a small glass of sherry

OR

a measure of vermouth or aperitif

These apply to the 25ml measure used in most of England and Wales. In some places, pub measures are larger than this. In Northern Ireland, a pub measure is 35ml – or 1¹/₂ units. In Scotland it can either be 35ml or 25ml. Take care—home measures are usually larger than these standard ones!

DRUGS

Any drugs may affect you or your growing baby — including illegal or street drugs. Always tell your doctor you are pregnant if you are prescribed any medication. If you buy medicines at the chemist's, ask the pharmacist if it's OK to take the product in pregnancy. Check the label yourself, as well.

- Cocaine, crack, heroin, amphetamines and cannabis, are known to affect a baby directly and indirectly. Crack and cocaine are especially dangerous, as they have an immediate effect on the baby's blood supply.

Babies of drug-dependent mothers are born dependent themselves, and suffer from withdrawal symptoms at birth.

- If you cannot stop using any drug, seek help. Some maternity units have specialist addiction units. Being pregnant may be the extra encouragement you need to cope with giving up. Your midwife, health visitor or antenatal clinic can put you in touch with support services, or speak to your family doctor. See also Further help at the back of this book.

Q. How can I avoid everything that might harm my baby? Exhaust fumes, pollution, radiation — they're everywhere. Is it possible to be completely safe?

A. You can't avoid everything that's harmful, but it makes sense to do what you can. The risk to your baby from smoking, for instance, is not just a theory. The effects have been demonstrated by good research. Worrying about aspects of your life which you can't control or avoid isn't very productive. It's worth remembering that the vast majority of babies are born strong and healthy.

Q. What about herbal medicine or homoeopathic remedies? And is aromatherapy safe?

A. Homoeopathic remedies are generally considered to be safe in pregnancy, but some herbal medicines and some aromatherapy oils are not suitable for pregnant women. Always get advice from a properly qualified practitioner. For minor complaints, there are useful books which will tell you what to avoid in pregnancy.

'Both of us have been smokers for about ten years, and I've never managed to give up for more than a few weeks before. This time, though, I think I will stay off. Joe has stopped smoking in the house, and I hope he'll soon stop completely... it's hard, but it's got to be worth trying.'

h e a l t h y c h o i c e s

Your partner can help you and your baby stay healthy by stopping smoking. If this isn't possible straight away, make a start by smoking away from the house only.

For more advice on smoking, alcohol or drugs see your midwife, GP or health visitor. If you want to stop smoking contact:

smokeline on 0800 84 84 84

for free information and support for you and for your partner.

Avoid X-rays in pregnancy if possible. This includes dental X-rays.

FEELING GOOD IN PREGNANCY

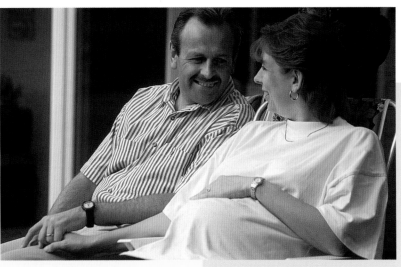

Sometimes you may feel tired, run down and uncomfortable. At other times, though, you'll feel you really know what people mean when they talk about the 'bloom' of pregnancy.

- Pregnancy hormones can change your skin and hair. Oily skin can become oilier, and dry skin can become drier, so skin care routines and hair care may change.

- From the fourth or fifth month, hormones affect the colour of your skin. The darker your skin, the more you'll notice it. If you have very fair skin and red hair, you may not. Nipples get darker, and the areola (the area around the nipple) gets bigger. A linea nigra ('black line') may appear down the midline of your chest and abdomen. Patchy colour may appear on your face. Using sunbeds is not advisable at any time but in pregnancy this patchy effect could be made worse by the sunbed. Be careful to use protection on your skin when outside in the sun.

- Stretchmarks are reddish-coloured stripes on the abdomen, breasts and thighs. They appear when the underlying tissues of the skin are stretched. After pregnancy, they gradually fade to a silvery-grey. The skin's elasticity is, to a large extent, inherited. Creams and lotions won't make much difference, although they are pleasant to use. Their moisturising effect keeps the surface of your skin free from itching and dryness.

Take care of your feet. You may be most comfortable in low-heeled or flat shoes. High heels can make any backache you have worse. Your feet may swell because your body retains more fluid, so you may need a wider fitting shoe, or even a half size larger. You may also have puffy ankles, and some aching. Some fluid retention is normal in pregnancy, but you should tell your midwife or doctor if there is any sudden increase.

feeling good

National Health Service (NHS) dental treatment, prescriptions and chiropody are free while you are pregnant (and for a year after the birth). However, you need a certificate, issued by your health board. Ask your midwife or family doctor.

EXERCISE IN PREGNANCY

Exercising to keep active and fit helps you feel well, so that you're in good physical condition for the birth. Exercise improves your heart's functioning and your circulation, which will help common complaints of pregnancy such as constipation, varicose veins or swelling (oedema). If you have backache, exercise and some attention to your posture can do a lot to relieve it.

Walking, swimming, some forms of yoga, or tone and stretch, can be done at any stage of pregnancy. It's best to avoid sports or exercise with a risk of falling, or hard physical contact with other players. Any exercises which 'bounce' your baby on your pelvic floor may also cause long-term damage to these muscles.

Swimming

Even if you haven't done much exercise before your pregnancy, you'll find swimming is easy. The water supports your whole body, so there's almost no risk of injury, and you can tone and stretch all over.

- Many pools run 'aquanatal' classes, where you learn movements and exercises designed for pregnancy. These should be run by a specially trained midwife, or an obstetric physiotherapist with a midwife present.

- In any class, you should be given the chance to warm up with some gentle limb stretches, followed by movements which work round the body, and maybe a swim.

questions Q&A answered

Q. I do aerobics twice or three times a week. Is it safe now I'm pregnant?

A. If you're already used to aerobics, then carry on. Tell your instructor you are pregnant, and avoid doing any exercises which risk straining your back. After about five months, concentrate on stretching and toning, without any jogging or jumping.

Remember to watch out for any exercises that might 'bounce' your baby onto your pelvic floor. Don't do any abdominal sit-up exercises. Stop before you feel really tired. This isn't the time for anyone to start doing this form of exercise.

Yoga

Yoga is generally a safe and helpful form of exercise in pregnancy. The poses gently stretch the body, and the breathing methods and emphasis on relaxation encourage peace and calm.

- If you belong to a class, tell the teacher you are pregnant. If you want to start yoga, it's best to find a teacher rather than try by yourself. Local authority adult education classes usually include yoga courses.

- Some of the very advanced poses will be beyond you in pregnancy, and you shouldn't attempt them. Just as with any exercise, stop if you feel any strain.

Loosen up!

Your pelvis needs to 'open up' to allow the baby to get through during labour and birth. To allow this, the ligaments in your pelvis soften and become more stretchable. Hormones, including relaxin, help this to happen.

Ligaments are bands of strong, elastic-like tissue connecting the bones of your skeleton at the joints. Because your ligaments soften in pregnancy, it's easy to stretch too far and end up straining a ligament — especially if you're not used to exercise. If you over-stretch you feel pain. This is your body telling you to stop.

Stand tall!

You can strengthen your back, and avoid backache, by learning to 'stand tall'. Stand with feet apart and let the weight of the body sink through to your feet. Imagine a string from the top of your head drawing you up towards the ceiling. Feel your spine lengthening.

- If you have to stand, remember this posture. It helps to stop you slumping and sagging into your tummy.

- If you sit for long periods, tuck a small cushion into the small of your back to help you sit straight and comfortably. This takes the strain away from your back.

exercise

Eating in pregnancy

FOODS TO CHOOSE, FOODS TO AVOID

Healthy eating in pregnancy is no different from healthy eating at any other time of your life. If you already eat well, you don't have to make any major changes in pregnancy. There are only a few, potentially important, points to watch in the foods you choose, and in the way you prepare your food before eating it. (See page 16 for further information on vegetarian and vegan diets.)

Foods to choose

Healthy eating doesn't mean you have to eat anything you don't enjoy. Aim to eat foods from each of these food groups:

- **bread, cereals, rice, pasta, potatoes** — these should make up the main part of every meal. Wholegrain cereal foods such as brown rice or wholemeal bread have more fibre and are more filling.

- **fruit and vegetables** — try to aim for five or more portions of fruit and vegetables per day. Use any kind, including fresh, frozen, tinned and dried, and pure fruit juices.

- **meat, fish and alternatives (these provide protein and iron)** — include some food from this group twice a day. This includes meat, chicken, fish (including tinned fish), eggs, nuts (see important note over the page), beans, pulses.

- **milk and dairy foods (these provide an important source of calcium)** — try to include one pint of milk per day or swap 1/3 of a pint of milk for 1oz of cheese (matchbox size), a yoghurt or a bowl of milk pudding. Low fat dairy products have the same amount of calcium as full fat varieties.

- **foods containing fat and foods containing sugar** — keep foods from this group to a minimum.

Foods to avoid

Some foods do carry risks in pregnancy. The risks are very small, so even if you do eat some of these foods, perhaps without realising, you are unlikely to harm yourself or your baby in any way. But it makes sense to avoid them if you can. Certain foods may be contaminated with bacteria such as listeria and salmonella.

Foods to avoid are:

- unpasteurised milks
- soft, ripened cheeses (such as brie, camembert and similar blue-veined varieties)
- liver and liver products (see page 15)
- pâtés — all types
- raw and undercooked eggs (cook until both the white and yolk are solid)
- ice-cream from soft whip machines.

    (**Note**: wrapped or block ice-cream is safe.)

If you or members of your close family suffer from peanut allergy or allergic disease such as atopic eczema, asthma or hayfever, it is recommended that you should avoid eating peanuts or foods containing peanut products during pregnancy and whilst breastfeeding.

GENERAL HYGIENE

- Always wash your hands before and after handling any food.

- Wash all fruit and vegetables thoroughly.

- Wash your hands after handling raw meat.

- Store raw foods separately from prepared foods.

- Always wear gloves and wash your hands thoroughly after gardening or handling soil.

CONTACT WITH ANIMALS

Some animals, particularly cats and sheep, may carry harmful micro-organisms including listeria, chlamydia psittaci or toxoplasma. These organisms can cause infection in pregnant women and cause harm to the unborn child.

- Always wash your hands after stroking your pet, especially before eating and preparing food.

- Try to keep pets out of the kitchen, and particularly off any surface on which you prepare food.

- Use separate dishes and utensils for preparing pet food and clean them separately from your family's.

- Keep your cat litter tray clean. Try to get someone else to dispose of soiled litter. If you have to handle it always wear rubber gloves **and** wash your hands and the gloves thoroughly afterwards.

- Always wear gloves when gardening in case cats have fouled in the garden. Wash your hands thoroughly afterwards.

Source: *While You Are Pregnant,* pp. 7–8, Department of Health, 1995.

FOLIC ACID

Folic acid is one of the important B vitamins. It's found naturally in many foods, and is added to some manufactured foods. This vitamin is vital for the growth and health of all the cells in the body. Folic acid is very important in the early stages of pregnancy, or if you are planning a pregnancy.

Women planning a pregnancy and pregnant women should take more folic acid to help prevent babies from being affected by 'neural tube defects' such as spina bifida.

Currently, it's recommended you take a 400 mcg (0.4 mg) folic acid tablet for at least three months before becoming pregnant and for 12 weeks into your pregnancy.

If you become pregnant unexpectedly, start taking a folic acid tablet every day until the twelfth week.

How to take it

If you are planning to become pregnant, or as soon as you know you are pregnant:

● start taking a daily supplement in the form of a 400 mcg folic acid tablet (the recommended dose), which your doctor may prescribe, or which you can buy in pharmacies and some supermarkets

and

● eat more foods that contain folic acid.

Avoid taking Vitamin A supplements as high levels could be harmful to the baby. Your doctor will prescribe vitamin supplements if you need them.

Foods with folic acid

● Green vegetables, including spinach, broccoli, green beans, cauliflower, Brussels sprouts, peas.

● Cereal foods, including bread. Some breads and breakfast cereals are fortified with folic acid — check the label.

● Some fruits, including oranges, grapefruit, bananas.

● Beans and pulses, especially black-eyed beans, chick peas.

● Milk and yoghurt.

● Yeast extracts (taken as a drink or a spread).

What about liver?

Liver contains folic acid but also has high levels of Vitamin A, which could be harmful to the baby in the early months of pregnancy. Pregnant women, and women planning a pregnancy, are advised not to eat liver, or liver products.

DIFFERENT TASTES?

Changes in how you feel about certain foods during your pregnancy is common. You may find you cannot take some foods and drinks which you previously enjoyed, like coffee or alcohol. Similarly you may find you have an increased liking for other foods, some of which you may not have enjoyed before becoming pregnant, eg citrus fruits and milk. Some women develop a taste for odd combinations of food. As long as you are eating a healthy balance of foods (see page 13) increasing the amount you eat of one food or cutting out another will not matter. If your craving is for very sweet or high fat foods, like chocolate, try to keep the amount you eat in moderation.

Q. **I was overweight before becoming pregnant. Is it okay to try to slim while I am pregnant?**

A. Don't aim to lose weight when you're pregnant. Instead, aim for a healthy balance of foods. Discuss this with your midwife or GP. Remember foods containing fat and foods containing sugar can provide a lot of calories (energy) and should be kept to a minimum.

Q. **Is a vegetarian or vegan diet safe in pregnancy?**

A. Yes, as long as you follow all the guidelines for healthy eating. All the nutrients you need are available in foods other than meat. Vegans — who eat no food from animal sources — may need extra Vitamin B12, and should choose foods such as soya products which have been fortified with Vitamin B12, or take supplements.

See also **Further help** at the back of this book.

Weeks up to 6

CONCEPTION AND EARLY PREGNANCY

This is the most 'active' part of your baby's development. A great deal happens in these first weeks — often before you know for sure you are pregnant.

- **The fertilised egg — now called a blastocyst — attaches itself to the womb lining** by the end of the first week after fertilisation. It burrows into the lining, and there is an exchange of chemicals and nutrients between the blastocyst and the lining.

- **When the blastocyst is well-implanted it is known as the embryo** and is about the same size as the full stop at the end of this sentence.

- **The outer cells of the embryo start to attach themselves to the mother's blood vessels,** linking in to the mother's blood supply. This is the beginning of the chorionic villi, which will become the placenta.

- **The inner cells of the embryo then divide into three separate layers.** The first layer will become the nervous system and brain; the second layer will become major internal organs (digestive system and lungs); the third layer will become the heart and the blood system, the muscles and the skeleton.

- **The embryo now has its own blood vessels.** Some of them connect with your own blood supply in the uterine wall. They develop into the umbilical cord, which contains the blood vessels taking nutrients from the placenta, and waste products from the baby.

When you are six weeks pregnant, this very complex organism is about the same size as the nail on your little finger.

Fertilised egg (blastocyst) dividing and moving along fallopian tube

Blastocyst implanting in womb lining, now an 'embryo'

Egg being fertilised by sperm

Egg being released from ovary

Right ovary

WEEKS 4–5

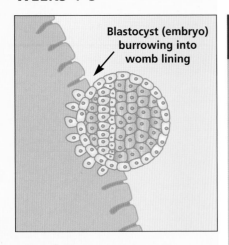

Blastocyst (embryo) burrowing into womb lining

You may have slight bleeding around the time when the egg implants itself into the wall of the uterus. It's easy to mistake this for a very light period, so you may not realise you are pregnant.

WEEK 6

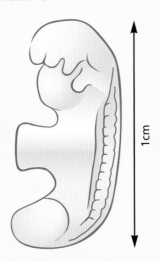

1cm

The baby's heartbeat can be detected on a scan as early as six or seven weeks.

questions answered **Q&A**

Q. Are pregnancy tests really all that reliable? I was sure I was pregnant, but the test showed negative. A week later I did it again and it was positive.

A. Pregnancy tests are usually reliable when used properly, though there is a small chance of a false negative. The tests you buy at the chemist's can pick up the hormone human chorionic gonadotrophin (HCG) in urine from about two weeks after conception ie at about the time when you would be due a period. But sometimes there may not be quite enough HCG present for the test to detect, which is why you should repeat the test if your period still doesn't come. This hormone can also be detected in a blood test.

OTHER SIGNS OF PREGNANCY

● Your cervix softens slightly.

● The vagina and the cervix change colour — from pink to purplish-blue — because of the increased blood supply in these areas.

● Your breasts start to change, and the tubercles (small, spot-like bumps) on the areola (area surrounding the nipple) become more prominent. These tubercles are the exit points of glands which produce an oily substance to keep the nipples supple and soft, in preparation for breastfeeding.

Take folic acid supplements for at least the first 12 weeks of pregnancy (see page 15).

Weeks 7–12

TAKING SHAPE

Now the embryo starts to develop a human body shape, and the major organs develop.

- Within a couple of weeks, there are small bumps called **limb buds**, which become arms and legs.

- By week 10, there is a larger, rounded end which will become the head. The umbilical cord has lengthened, and the embryo is floating inside the **amniotic sac** (the 'bag of waters' which protects the baby throughout the pregnancy).

- At the end of this time, the embryo is called a **fetus**. Facial features start to form — mouth, tongue and eyelids. The limb buds are now recognisable arms and legs, with the beginnings of the fingers and toes. Important work in forming the internal organs, the brain and the nervous system and the skeleton happens in these weeks. By the end of 12 weeks, the structure of the internal organs is complete, and the muscles begin to develop. At the end of week 12, the baby measures about 5 cm (1.9 inches) from head to bottom — the size of a ripe plum.

- By 12 weeks you may find your waistline is already thickening. The organs in the pelvis are being slightly displaced as your uterus moves upwards. You may have some fluid retention, too, which makes you feel fuller around your middle. You won't look pregnant to most people, though.

SICKNESS AND NAUSEA

In the first 12 weeks, sickness and nausea may be at its worst. You may feel very tired, too. You are likely to feel better soon. Hormones change at about 12 to 14 weeks, when the placenta starts working, and most women feel better after this.

feeling better

What to do

- Keep meals small and frequent, so your stomach always has something in it.

- Start the day with a dry cracker and a drink — even before you get out of bed.

- Sipping something fizzy such as a soft drink or a gassy mineral water throughout the day seems to help some women. Ask your GP or your midwife for more suggestions.

WEEK 9

WEEK 12

The fetus is becoming more human in appearance.

2 cm (less than an inch)

Weeks 13–16

The placenta starts to take over as the main source of nourishment for the baby from week 13. It functions fully by week 14.

YOUR BABY'S FEATURES

- At the beginning of these weeks, the baby has some independent movement of the limbs and the head, though you won't feel it yet. You might feel some movement at 16 weeks, often later in first pregnancies.

- By week 16, your baby's face has clearly-marked eyes, nose, mouth and ears. The eyelids have developed, and the teeth are inside the gums.

- There is a soft, fine covering of hair all over the body, called 'lanugo'.

- If your baby is going to have dark hair, the cells of the hair follicles which produce colour begin to work from week 15.

- Eyebrows and eyelashes also start to grow. Fingernails and toenails are there. The eyes and ears continue to develop, and we know babies at this stage are aware of sound and light.

At week 16, your baby is 8 cm (about 3 inches) in length.

THE PLACENTA

This is your baby's life-support system. It is attached to the uterus on one side, and to the baby by the umbilical cord on the other. The umbilical cord brings nutrients from the mother's blood via the placenta to the baby and carries waste products away. The placenta also produces hormones which circulate around your body.

Your bloodstream and your baby's never normally come into direct contact. Your blood bathes the side of the placenta attached to the uterus wall. Nutrients, including oxygen, pass through a membrane which separates your bloodstream from the baby's, then into the baby's bloodstream on the other side of the placenta. Waste products from the baby are dealt with in the same way, passing from the baby's side to your side through the membrane.

The placenta filters out many hazards before they can reach the baby. However, some harmful substances can still get through the barrier. The placenta can't 'block' some bacteria, viruses, drugs, some medicines, nicotine and carbon monoxide.

The hormones produced by the placenta — mainly oestrogen and progesterone — bring about many of the changes you can observe in your body during pregnancy.

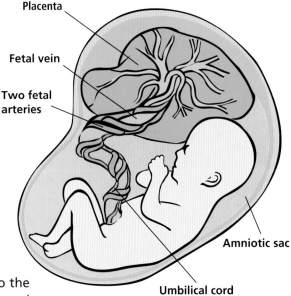

Placenta

Fetal vein

Two fetal arteries

Amniotic sac

Umbilical cord

They affect the growth of your uterus and cause new blood vessels to develop. At the end of pregnancy, the levels of progesterone produced by the placenta fall, but it is not entirely clear what is responsible for starting labour.

Weeks 17–20

YOUR 'BUMP' SHOWS

During these weeks, you start to look pregnant, although women who are very slim and who have a small 'bump' may not look very different, especially if they wear loose clothing.

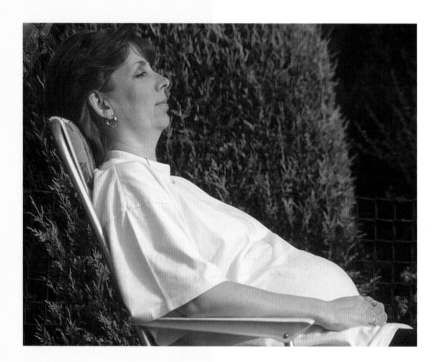

- Around now, you will probably feel the baby's first movements — though you may not be sure that's what they are, especially if you have never been pregnant before. The movements (known as 'quickening') feel fluttery at first, but as time goes on you will feel them as definite pokes and prods, as your baby's movements touch the inside of your abdomen.

- Ultrasound pictures have shown babies of about 18 weeks sucking their thumbs.

- Your baby's second teeth begin to form, behind the start of the first teeth. The baby's body begins to be covered in 'vernix', a greasy substance which coats your baby's skin forming a waterproof layer.

- At 20 weeks, your baby is 15 cm in length (about 6 inches), still small enough to curl into an adult hand.

WEEK 20

WORKING DURING PREGNANCY

Most pregnant women are able to work as long as they want to. However, a very few jobs may be unsafe or ill-advised when you're pregnant.

- If you work with **chemicals**, for example, or other dangerous substances, or if your job involves **climbing, or lifting heavy weights**, you may have to switch the tasks you do for something safer. Ask your midwife or doctor for their advice.

- **Your employer has a legal obligation** to make sure the work you do, and your working conditions, will not put your health, or your baby's, at risk. If there is a risk, he or she must offer you alternative employment.

- **You are entitled to paid time off** to attend antenatal appointments and antenatal classes. (You may have to produce a note from your doctor or midwife stating that these classes are considered to be part of your antenatal care.)

- **Start thinking about benefits**, if you haven't already, and about whether or not you intend to go back to work after your baby's born. You can find sources of information about money matters and your maternity rights in the Further help section at the back of this book. (See also page 57).

Weeks 21–24

CHANGING SHAPE

At this time, your uterus grows rapidly and you may gain quite a bit of weight. At about 24 weeks, you'll notice your tummy button flattening, or even popping out, with the pressure from the growing uterus beneath.

MEASURING THE BABY

During antenatal appointments, the midwife or doctor may measure your tummy with a tape. They will also feel (palpate) your tummy with their hands to check the baby's size and growth. The position will be noted. Babies change their position all the time, right up to a few weeks before the birth.

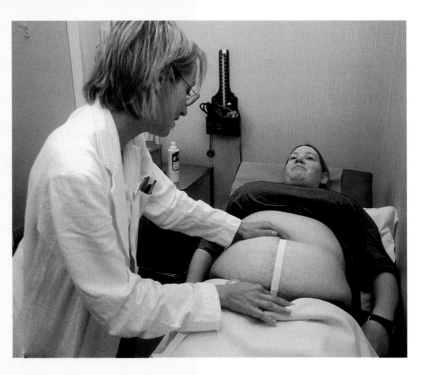

FEELING BETTER

Many women begin to feel energetic and fit, as the tiredness common in early pregnancy goes, and you don't yet feel the heaviness of late pregnancy. Although you may feel tired, you'll probably sleep well and wake refreshed. Your body is doing a lot of unseen work — for example, your heart and lungs are actually working 50 per cent harder than when you're not pregnant.

MATERNITY CLOTHES — DO YOU NEED THEM?

After about four or five months, you won't fit into many of your ordinary clothes, as your waist thickens, and your breasts get larger. If you buy clothes, try to choose things you can wear afterwards — roomy, loose tops, sweaters and T-shirts. You may find you need to buy one or two special items in the very last weeks, if you get very big. Here are some more ideas pregnant

women have suggested to help:

- **maternity leggings** are a good buy — you can wear them after the birth, too, replacing the elastic in the waistband if necessary with a shorter length

- **large T-shirts, shirts and jumpers**. Men's sizes are roomy and comfortable if you don't mind rolling up extra long sleeves

- **wear ordinary tights** (cheaper than maternity ones) but buy them in extra large sizes and wear them back to front, so the larger part of the pants is over your tummy

- **most women feel more comfortable in a bra**, even if they don't normally wear one. Get measured for a maternity bra at about seven months. Nursing bras have cups which unhook or unzip, and are helpful for breastfeeding later.

Weeks 25–28

YOUR BABY'S MOVING

Your baby's body gradually looks more in proportion and baby-like during these weeks.

- You'll feel your baby move a lot more, and you may see movements if you lie still in the bath. You might even be able to make out which movements come from a hand or a foot, especially later on, when the uterus is larger.

- The skin is less transparent now and starts to thicken. Babies of this age have hardly any fat under their skin, so it is wrinkled and loose. Creases appear on the palms of the hands and the soles of feet, and by the end of 25 weeks fingerprints form.

- Although not common for a variety of reasons, some babies can be born at this stage. Today, with specialist care, babies can survive outside the uterus from as early as 24 weeks of pregnancy. Great progress has been made in this area of medicine in the last few years. However, at this early stage many babies who survive can have long-term problems.

Survival rates increase week-by-week after this time. Most babies born at 28 weeks survive without long-term problems, though they still need weeks of special care.

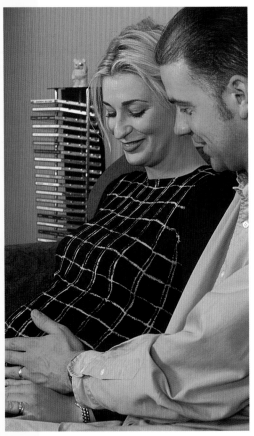

- At 28 weeks, your baby is about 22 cm long (8½ inches), and weighs 800 grams (about one-and-half pounds).

CHANGES

- Your breasts produce **colostrum** (a thick, creamy substance) at this time, though you may not be aware of it. This is the first fluid made in your breasts (see page 100). Some women leak a little. If you notice this, it's nothing to worry about. It will dry into small crusts on your nipples, so just wash this off with plain water.

- There may be some **oedema** (swelling) of your feet and hands. This is very common from 26 weeks or so onwards. You should point it out next time you see your midwife or doctor. It's not likely to be anything more serious than the normal fluid retention of pregnancy (see page 53). But severe oedema plus high blood pressure and protein in the urine would suggest you have pre-eclampsia (see pages 55–56) and this is more important.

questions Q&A answered

Q. I get very stressed at work, and sometimes at home, too. I then feel guilty in case my baby picks it up.

A. If you are feeling very stressed or tired, then do take steps to reduce it. You might benefit from resting more, or leaving work early. Or begin your maternity leave sooner than you planned. Recent research shows that high stress levels in pregnancy may affect some aspects of your baby's development, and may also be linked with breathing problems at birth.

YOUR BABY CAN HEAR

Your baby's ears are very sensitive from the 24th week of pregnancy. Inside the uterus, your heartbeat, the noises of your digestive system, your voice and other voices are all heard by your baby. It's well-known that the regular sound of something like a heartbeat can calm a crying newborn. A baby who cries a lot may find womb noises soothing (you can buy a tape).

Weeks 29–32

TIRED AND UNCOMFORTABLE?

From week 30 or so, your baby's body gradually fills out as he or she lays down fat underneath the skin. By 30 weeks, the hair on the face and body will start to disappear, but the 'vernix' (see page 22) remains.

Baby boys' testes may descend from their abdomen towards the top of the scrotum from about week 29.

- Now you may start to feel the pressure on your stomach and under your ribs, and on your bladder. This means it can be harder to get into a position where you can breathe easily while lying or sitting, and it means you may need to pass urine more often.

- The skin on your abdomen will feel thin and stretched. This is the time when you might see your first stretchmarks, if you're going to get them (see page 10).

- Stay at work if you want to, as long as your job, or travelling to and from it, is not too physically demanding. Check with your midwife if you're not sure about this. You might prefer to be at home, preparing for your baby

and enjoying the free time you have left if this is your first baby. It may be the longest time to yourself you'll have for quite some time!

- Backache may be more of a problem at this time, as the increasing size of your abdomen draws you forward.

- Your antenatal checks are likely to continue fortnightly at about this time. Some women have an ultrasound scan at some time during these weeks, mainly to see the growth and development of your baby, and to see if the major organs are as they should be.

SEX IN PREGNANCY

Sex is normally perfectly safe in pregnancy. Any sexual activity that doesn't harm you will not harm your baby. You don't risk 'jostling', hurting or affecting your baby. The baby is protected in the uterus by the bag of waters, which cushions movement. The baby may feel the movements of vigorous sexual activity, but they won't do any harm.

Is it ever risky?

Occasionally, women who have had a number of miscarriages might be advised not to have sex around about the time their period would have been due, or even at all during the first three months. There's no evidence that sex and miscarriage are linked, though, and there is some disagreement among doctors about how to advise couples in this situation.

- Some women feel that sex with man or woman on top positions is a little uncomfortable in later pregnancy. You can get round this by the person on top bearing their weight on their arms. Or, try side-by-side positions.

- Some women — and some men — get less keen on penetrative sex as the pregnancy develops. That's fine. You can have closeness and as much sexual excitement as you want without it.

- Women, like men, sometimes find their desire for sex changes in pregnancy, and both men and women may go off it, too.

None of this can mean anything serious, or long-lasting. Try to keep your closeness with lots of warm, physical contact that need not lead to sex. If it played an important role in your lives before, then the feelings are very likely to come back in time.

Your antenatal care appointments have probably been about every four weeks, but they may become fortnightly now, and you may have stopped work. Many antenatal or parentcraft classes start about now (see pages 64–65).

BABIES BORN EARLY: YOUR BABY IN SPECIAL CARE

Babies born before 37 weeks are called 'pre-term' (more usual these days than 'premature'). They usually need some time in the hospital's special or intensive care baby unit. Intensive care is for sicker or weaker babies, who need more medical and nursing support.

- The outlook for pre-term babies is better than it used to be, but being born too soon does bring problems. The main hazards are infection and difficulties with breathing.

- It can be hard to feel your baby is really yours while in an incubator, attached to electrodes and tubes. If your baby is very sick, or very pre-term, you may even be wary of getting too close emotionally, fearing, perhaps, that your baby may not survive.

- You can do a great deal for your baby, though. Even the tiniest pre-term babies can sometimes be cuddled for short times outside the incubator. Touching, stroking, talking to your baby, whether inside or outside the incubator, is important. Studies show that babies who have this sort of loving contact put on weight more quickly. As soon as you can, hold your baby close, with plenty of skin-to-skin contact.

- Staff can explain the machines involved in your baby's care. Some of the equipment simply measures responses and functions, such as breathing, body temperature and heart rate.

- Some babies may be too small or weak to feed from the breast. If you plan to breastfeed later, you can express your milk. This helps to establish a milk supply by stimulating your breasts to produce milk. It also means that your baby can take milk through a feeding tube, or perhaps from a little cup. You can hand express or use an electric breast pump (see page 106).

- You may not get very much milk at first, but tiny babies only need very small amounts. Your milk is very valuable, as the **antibodies** in it help your baby fight infection. The colostrum which the breasts produce in the first days is especially nutritious.

For further information turn to page 67.

29

Weeks 33–36

GETTING READY

Your baby puts on about 200 grams a week (about seven ounces) in these weeks, growing bigger and laying down more fat.

● After about 33 weeks, you may sometimes feel jerky movements. This is thought to be the baby having a mild attack of hiccups.

● By 36 weeks, most babies (about 95 per cent) are head-down in the uterus, in the position known as 'cephalic'. First babies engage in the pelvis at about this time. The head descends into the pelvis, fitting in quite firmly. Second or later babies tend to engage later (this is because the pelvic bones are arranged

slightly differently after a pregnancy and birth). For more information about engagement, see page 32.

● At 36 weeks, your baby measures about 44 cm (18 inches) and weighs 2500 grams (about five-and-a-half pounds).

Packing your bag: some ideas

A few weeks before your expected day of delivery, check that you have the right things to take with you into hospital. It might help to have three bags — one for labour, one for after the birth and one for going home. Your midwife or antenatal clinic may give you a suggestions sheet. If not, here are some.

Bag one (labour)

● Drinks and snacks for you and your partner.

● Mineral water spray or a plant spray with a fine nozzle. Put it in a fridge (if you have access to one) to keep it cool.

● Two facecloths for cooling your face and skin.

● Music tapes and a cassette player (battery operated).

● Oil or a light body lotion for massage.

● Thermal pack (the sort you can heat in a microwave for taking with you on cold outings or on a picnic — it stays warm for hours). It can be wrapped in a towel and used as a warm compress to relieve aches in the back or in the legs.

● Old nightdress (front-opening for easy breastfeeding) or old T-shirt.

● Dressing-gown (robe) and sandals or slippers.

● Pair of socks.

● Hair brush.

● Hair bands for long hair.

● Wash bag with toiletries and flannel.

● Phone card/coins.

Preparing for a home birth

If you are planning a home birth your midwife will have a special delivery pack which she will drop off at your house some time before your baby is due. It contains things like sterile cloths and swabs. She will bring her own equipment to the birth. Ask her what she wants you to provide.

Bag two
(after the birth)

- Two nightdresses (front-opening for easy breastfeeding).
- Easy-to-wear dayclothes (like a jogging suit).
- Underwear, including large, close fitting pants (to hold maternity pads), and nursing bras.
- Towels.
- Maternity pads or night-time sanitary pads. (Large disposable nappies may be better for 24 hours after the birth.)
- Breast pads (to absorb leaks of colostrum and milk).
- Tissues.
- Phone card/coins.
- Toiletries and cosmetics.
- Nappies for baby.
- Something to read.
- Notepaper, pens, stamps and envelopes.
- Pack of biscuits or other snacks.
- Fruit juice/mineral water.

Bag three
(to go home)

- Baby clothes.
- Clothes for you.

You will need a car seat for the journey home.

Q. My midwife has told me that my baby is in a 'posterior' position. She said that this may make my labour longer and that I will probably get backache. What is a posterior position, and can I do something about it?

A. A posterior position is when your baby's back is lying against your back. This position probably does not matter right now, but later, when you go into labour, your baby has to turn all the way around to the front. Whilst in this position his or her head presses against your sacrum (lower back) and can cause backache. However, there are some things you can do before your baby is born which may help.

From about 36 weeks you might want to try using leaning forward positions whenever you can. This usually helps your baby to turn so that her back is towards your front, before her head becomes lodged in your pelvis. (Ideally, if this is your first baby, the back should also be to your left side.)

Possible things you could do:
- keep your knees lower than your hips
- keep your back above your tummy.

So, whenever you relax in front of the television, lean forward over a beanbag or lie on your left side on the couch. Whilst driving you can put a small cushion under the back of your bottom. If you have a posture seat, with knee rests, use it as much as you can. These adjustments to your posture can encourage your baby to turn the right way.

Weeks 37–40 plus

UP TO THE BIRTH DAY

These last weeks may seem to go slowly. Don't think of your baby as being 'due' on a certain day — many babies are later than this.

- At any time after week 36 or so, your baby's head may move well down into the pelvis. This is called 'engagement' (see opposite). You may now feel it's easier to breathe as your uterus exerts less pressure on your diaphragm. This is why the sensation you get is called 'lightening'.

- You'll probably feel different movements this late in pregnancy, as there is so little room in the uterus for the baby. Movements are more likely to feel 'big' rather than a series of smaller kicks. Your baby quite naturally has sleep times and wakeful times, so a quiet period may mean no more than a longish nap. However, contact the hospital, the midwife or the doctor if you don't feel your baby moving for several hours.

- The baby's lungs are maturing all the time, and she or he practises light breathing movements.

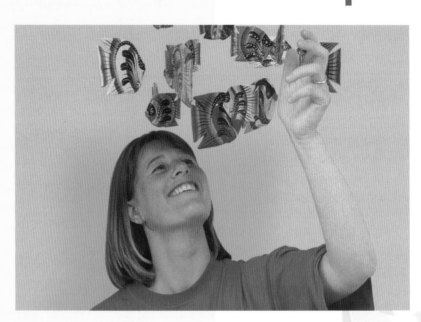

In the last two weeks of pregnancy, your baby may have a final growth spurt. At term, the average baby weighs between 3 and 4 kg (about 6 to 8 pounds) and measures about 35 to 37 cm (14–15 inches) long.

ENGAGEMENT

- Engagement of the head means that the largest diameter of the baby's head has passed the pelvic 'brim'. This means that the baby will fit through the pelvis and a normal birth should be possible. This happens most easily when the crown of the baby's head is coming first and the head is well 'curled' under. If this is not the case and the baby's head is in the posterior position (see page 31), or even if the 'brow' or 'face' is presenting, the head cannot fit into the pelvis.

- In many cases, and especially with posterior positions and in second or subsequent babies, when labour starts the baby's head will rotate and curl under with the power of the contractions. This means that the baby's head will fit into the pelvis and a normal birth will be possible. This is why in most cases it is wise to see what happens in labour (a 'trial of labour') rather than assume that there is disproportion — where the pelvis is too small for the baby's head, or its shape is not ideal — and have a planned Caesarean section. Sometimes, however, the head will not rotate or the pelvis will be definitely too small and a Caesarean section will be required.

ARE THESE 'REAL' CONTRACTIONS?

The uterus is formed of a network of strong muscle fibres, and contracts all the way through pregnancy. You may not be aware of this until later in your pregnancy (from 28 weeks onwards). The contractions can then be very noticeable. They are called **Braxton Hicks** contractions, and it can be easy to mistake them for labour.

You will feel your abdomen harden, and if you are in the bath, say, you will see it harden and remain tense for a number of seconds. Unlike labour contractions, Braxton Hicks contractions don't increase in length, intensity and frequency. They tend to be short, and come and go intermittently. Time them, and this will help you decide if it's the real thing or not.

Week 40

Q. **My baby is breech. What does this mean?**

A. It means that your baby is lying head-up in the uterus. His or her bottom is probably the part that will be born first — the presenting part. Occasionally, a foot is nearest the cervix (known as a footling breech).

Babies may lie with their legs bent at the knees, almost 'cross-legged', or with their legs straight up towards the face. This is known as a frank breech.

Q. **How common is breech presentation?**

A. At 30 weeks of pregnancy, about 20 per cent of babies are in the breech position. By term, the figure is down to three per cent. Many babies move into a head-down (vertex) position by themselves.

Q. **Does it affect the birth?**

A. It can. Being born head first is usually easier and quicker. Babies who are still breech by about 36 weeks of pregnancy may not turn by themselves, so some doctors do a manoeuvre called external cephalic version (ECV) to try to get them to turn.

Q. **Will I need a Caesarean section?**

A. Not necessarily. Some obstetricians prefer to deliver breech babies with a Caesarean section but many are born vaginally. Talk it over with your midwife and the consultant.

Q. **Why am I more likely to need a Caesarean section?**

A. The largest part of a baby is the head, and if the head is too large for the mother's pelvis, then it will not pass through. If the baby is coming head first then the problem will become obvious during labour. However, if the baby is breech, then the baby's bottom, which is smaller than its head, might pass through the pelvis and it will be more difficult to know if the head will fit safely through and not be damaged. Obstetricians are therefore reluctant to advise a 'trial of labour' if they have any concern at all that the baby's head will fit.

Antenatal care

WHERE AND WHAT TO EXPECT

Your antenatal care aims to check that you and your baby are well, and to pick up any problems before they become serious.

Where?

You'll probably have between 8 and 15 appointments. A few may be at the hospital antenatal clinic, but most of them will take place in the midwives' or GP's clinic, or at home.

What to expect?

The booking appointment is the first major appointment, usually at about 8 to 12 weeks. You'll be asked a lot of questions to get a good picture of your health, and you'll be asked where you want to have your baby, so that a place can be booked for you (see page 47). You

can change your mind later. You can also ask questions yourself, of course, as this is an important chance for you to find out what you want to know. (See page 64 for information about antenatal classes.)

YOUR RECORDS

Your notes are the written record of your antenatal care. They have information about any previous pregnancies, and letters from any of the health professionals involved in your care. The results of any tests are also included.

You may carry your own notes, or they may be held at the doctor's, midwives' or hospital clinic. Instead of notes, you may look after the shared care card. This is a smaller version of your notes, containing the basic information about you and your pregnancy. Each time you have an antenatal appointment, the health professional you see records observations on the card, and signs it.

Take your notes/card with you if you go away from home for any length of time, in case you need to consult a doctor or a midwife. You are entitled to see a full copy of your notes at any time, before or after birth.

WORDS YOU MAY COME ACROSS

Here are some of the more common words you may come across when you read your notes, or overhear people talking:

ABORTION:
any pregnancy that ended before 24 weeks. A miscarriage is sometimes termed a 'spontaneous abortion'.

AFP:
alphafetoprotein. A substance present in the blood of pregnant women. Levels apparently higher or lower than normal may indicate the need for further tests (see pages 41–43).

ALB:
albumin, a protein substance. Your urine is tested for albumin, as it can be a sign of pre-eclampsia (see pages 55–56).

AMNIOTIC FLUID:
sometimes known as liquor (pronounced 'lye-kwor'). The fluid surrounding the baby in the uterus.

ANTENATAL:
before the birth.

APH:
antepartum haemorrhage — bleeding before birth.

BR:
breech presentation. A baby who is lying bottom or feet down in the uterus (the position of most babies until later pregnancy).

CEPH:
cephalic. The position of a baby who is lying head down in the uterus.

DIAPHRAGM:
muscle which lies across top of stomach, under lungs (active in pushing baby out).

ECTOPIC PREGNANCY:
a pregnancy which develops somewhere other than the uterus, usually in the fallopian tube. The pregnancy must be terminated, as it is dangerous to the mother.

EDD:
expected date of delivery.

ENG:
engaged. Means that the largest diameter of the baby's head has passed the pelvic 'brim'.

EPISIOTOMY:
a cut made in the perineum (the skin between the vagina and the anus) to enable the baby to be born more quickly (see page 81).

FETUS:
medical term for the baby before it is born, ie when still in the uterus.

FH:
fetal heart. You may see 'FH heard' or 'FHH' on your notes. It means your baby's heartbeat has been heard.

FM:
fetal movement. You may see 'FM felt' or 'FMF' on your notes. It means your baby has been felt to move.

FUNDUS:
the top of the uterus. The fundal height is the length between the top of the uterus and the pubic bone. This helps date the pregnancy and assess the growth of the baby.

Hb:
haemoglobin. An indication of iron levels in the blood. If this is too low, this may indicate anaemia.

HYPERTENSION:
high blood pressure.

HYPOTENSION:
low blood pressure.

LIE:
the position of the baby in the uterus. You may see 'Long Lie' or 'LL' which

means longitudinal lie (the baby is straight up and down in the uterus).

MULTIGRAVIDA:
a woman who has had at least one pregnancy.

MULTIPARA:
sometimes called 'multip'. A woman who has given birth at least once before. A 'grand multipara' is a woman who has had at least four babies.

NAD:
'nothing abnormal detected', written when the doctor or midwife finds no problems.

OCCIPITO ANTERIOR:
the back of the baby's head is towards your front. You may see LOA or ROA on your notes, which mean 'left (or right) occipito anterior'. This describes whether the back of the head is towards the left or the right. LOA is usually the best position for a shorter labour and an easier birth.

OCCIPITO POSTERIOR:
the back of the baby's head is towards your back. LOP and ROP describe the position as left or right.

OEDEMA:
fluid retention, which causes swelling in your ankles, fingers and elsewhere.

PALPATION:
when the midwife or doctor feels the baby by moving their hands over your abdomen.

PERINEUM:
the area of skin between the vagina and the anus.

PIH:
pregnancy-induced hypertension (see page 39).

PLACENTA PRAEVIA:
when the placenta is low down. Sometimes it covers the cervix and blocks the baby's exit.

POSTNATAL:
after the birth.

PRESENTATION:
the position of the baby, with reference to the 'presenting part', that is the body part which will be born first (usually the vertex, or the back of the head).

PRE-TERM:
born before 37 weeks of pregnancy.

PRIMIGRAVIDA:
a woman pregnant for the first time.

PRIMIPARA:
sometimes called 'prim' or a 'primip' — a woman giving birth for the first time.

QUICKENING:
the first movements of the baby you can feel (see page 22).

Rh:
Rhesus (see page 40).

SUTURE:
the spaces between the bones in the baby's head.

TERM:
40 weeks (or thereabouts) from the first day of the last menstrual period.

VE:
vaginal examination.

VENTOUSE:
vacuum extraction (see pages 80–81).

VX:
vertex. The crown of the baby's head.

PEOPLE YOU'LL MEET

Caring for you and your baby

At the hospital, during antenatal care and if you plan to have your baby there, you may meet several different health professionals and others. Here's who they are, and what they do:

midwife — qualified in the care of mothers and babies during normal pregnancy and childbirth, and in the early days after the birth. Midwives are trained to recognise potential problems. There are hospital midwives, and community midwives who work outside the hospital. Community midwives may visit you at home before the birth, and will certainly visit after the birth.

caring for you

obstetrician — a specialist doctor in pregnancy and childbirth. You may see an obstetrician, or another qualified doctor who is training in obstetrics, if there is a problem with your pregnancy or birth, and maybe if everything is okay, too.

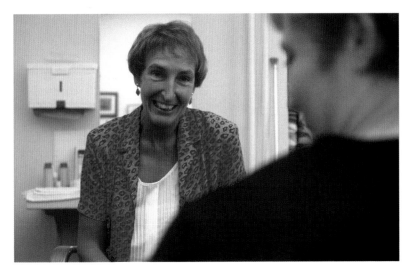

GP/family doctor — a doctor, who may also have an additional qualification in obstetrics. You can change your maternity care to a GP with this qualification, if you prefer. You may also see a GP Registrar, a qualified doctor gaining experience in general practice.

health visitor — a nurse who has undertaken extra training in child development and health promotion and who works in the community, either with a GP or according to a specific area. She or he gives support and advice to mothers and their children under five. This is your main source of information on child health and development shortly after the birth. You can visit your health visitor at the baby clinic, and he or she may come to meet you for the first time while you are still pregnant.

Note: health visitors and midwives may be male or female.

social worker — can help with advice and information on state benefits, and on housing difficulties, child care problems and so on.

dietitian — ask for advice if you have special dietary needs, whether connected with your pregnancy or not.

obstetric physiotherapist — may help you with postnatal exercises and possibly antenatal exercises, too. May be at parentcraft classes (see page 64).

paediatrician — a doctor who specialises in babies and children. If there are any worries about your baby's health, a paediatrician may be present at the birth. A paediatrician may also check your baby over before you go home from hospital.

radiographer — a technician who operates the ultrasound scanning equipment (see page 44).

radiologist — a doctor who specialises in ultrasound and X-rays.

q u e s t i o n s Q&A a n s w e r e d

Q. I am having some of my antenatal care at a teaching hospital. Will I have to have students looking after me?

A. No. Sometimes, students may observe what happens in an antenatal appointment, and labour and birth, or treat you, under supervision. Students need to learn on 'real' people, of course, but only if you agree first. You should be asked for your permission. If you don't want this, then that is fine. Simply say no. You don't have to say why.

If anyone involved in your care is undertaking research and wants to use your experience as part of the project, then you should be asked for your permission first. Again, you can say no if you prefer not to take part.

'Who are you?'

Health professionals should make a point of introducing themselves when they meet you — 'Good morning, I'm midwife Chris Smith/Doctor Sam Brown, etc.' If you don't catch the name, ask again, or see if they are wearing a name badge.

If anyone comes to your house saying they have come to see about your antenatal care (or anything else connected with your pregnancy) and you don't recognise them, ask to see identification. If you still have doubts, don't let them in. Ask them to come back later or on another day. This will give you time to make sure they are genuine. The same applies after the birth, too, when anyone calls saying they have come to see you and your baby. Don't let them in unless you're sure about who they are.

Some areas offer care based on 'team midwifery'. This means the same team of midwives share the same clients. It means you are more likely to get to know, and feel comfortable with, a small number of midwives, and they are more likely to get to know you.

ANSWERS TO YOUR QUESTIONS: ANTENATAL CARE

- Many mothers find it's helpful to **write down their questions**, and then to read them at the appointment. No-one will mind if you do this — health professionals know that it can be difficult to remember all you want to ask.

- You may prefer to **talk after your examination** — even if the health professional says 'Anything you'd like to ask?' during it. Lying down is not the best position to talk! Just say, 'Yes, I have one or two things, can I ask them afterwards?'

- **If there's anything you don't understand, ask.** You're bound to find things in your notes that puzzle you. Never worry that your question might sound trivial or make you appear silly. Doctors and midwives know it's important to have as much information as you want. You'll find a guide to some of the terms you may come across on page 35.

CHECKS AND TESTS DURING YOUR PREGNANCY

Always ask the reason for tests — they may be routine and straightforward to the health professionals carrying them out, but not to you. Some tests are not offered to all women — talk to your midwife or doctor about these tests (see below).

Routine tests

Blood tests

You'll probably be offered at least one blood test in pregnancy, taken at your first appointment. This can:

- identify your blood group
- see whether your blood is Rhesus positive or negative (see page 40)

- check for illnesses or conditions, such as anaemia, that could affect your, or your baby's, health (this may or may not include HIV — ask. If it does, you should be told about it and asked for your agreement).

Usually, a blood test means no more than taking a little blood from a vein in your arm. The blood is drawn up through a needle into a syringe. A blood test shouldn't be painful, though there may be slight bruising for a day or so afterwards.

Blood pressure

Your blood pressure is checked at most appointments. This is to make sure you have no signs of **pre-eclampsia**, or **pregnancy-induced hypertension** (see pages 55–56). The midwife or doctor wraps a fabric band around your arm and inflates it with a small pump. The cuff is linked to a blood pressure measure. As the cuff deflates, the midwife or doctor uses a stethoscope to listen to changes of your pulse.

A high reading may give cause for concern, so some health professionals will do the test again, 10 or 20 minutes later, to make doubly sure.

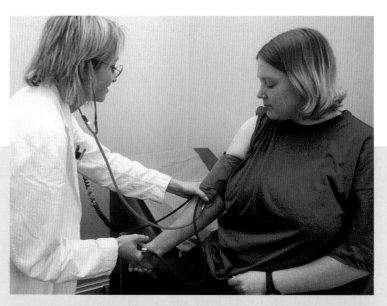

Urine

Your urine will be tested for **protein** and **sugar.** (A special strip is dipped into a sample which you either bring with you or produce at the appointment.) Some women develop a particular sort of diabetes that occurs in pregnancy — **gestational diabetes**. This might first show as sugar in the urine. Protein might indicate pre-eclampsia. Infections of the kidney and bladder might show up here, too.

Abdomen

Your abdomen will be **palpated** at each visit. This means the doctor or midwife feels the way your baby is lying, and its size, and the height of your uterus, by moving her hands around the outside of your abdomen.

questions Q&A answered

Q. **I have Rhesus negative blood, and I have been told I need injections to prevent my baby from being harmed. Can you explain?**

A. **Most people (80 per cent) have Rhesus positive blood (written in notes as Rh+ or Rh+ve). If you have Rhesus negative blood, and the father of your baby has Rhesus negative blood, too, there's no problem because your baby will have the same type. If you have Rhesus negative blood and the father is Rhesus positive, then your baby could be positive, which might cause a problem.**

In a first pregnancy your bloodstream and your baby's don't usually meet until the birth. Then they may come into contact when the placenta is delivered. As a result, in a second or subsequent pregnancy, your blood will produce antibodies which could cause a serious blood disorder in your baby. To avoid this, you will be offered injections of Anti-D gammaglobulin after your pregnancy, or during it if you have any bleeding. In some areas, Rhesus negative women may be offered injections during pregnancy whether or not there has been bleeding.

Screening and diagnostic tests in pregnancy

Some mothers may be offered tests which aren't appropriate for everyone. You can choose whether or not to have them, and you may want to discuss this with your midwife or doctor.

- A **screening test** aims to tell you if there is a risk that you or your baby may have a problem.

- A **diagnostic** test is done to show whether a problem actually exists. Many tests are useful, and some are very important, but no test is perfect — it may miss the thing it is designed to look for, (a 'false negative'), or it may seem to show something that isn't there (a 'false positive').

c a r i n g f o r y o u

Screening tests

Double test

After 15 weeks of pregnancy, you may be offered a blood test called a **double test**. It tests for the substances AFP and HCG. The test assesses the risk of Down's syndrome, spina bifida or other neural tube defects (NTDs). It's a screening test, and does not diagnose anything.

A higher or lower level than normal of one or more of these substances can mean an increased risk of the baby having these conditions. The testers also need to know the number of weeks you are pregnant (to calculate the risk for NTDs) and your age (to calculate the risk for Down's syndrome).

The result takes about 10 days, and you are told what risk you have of having a baby with a particular condition.

With chromosomal disorders such as Down's syndrome (see later), the result may be expressed as a 'one in something' chance. So, if you are told your result is a 'one in 400', it means your baby has a 1 in 400 chance of being affected by the disability. That is, for every 400 pregnancies with the same result, 399 are likely to be normal.

Diagnostic tests

Depending on the results of screening tests, you may be offered a further test, such as **amniocentesis**, or **ultrasound**, which aim to diagnose any problem. In most cases, these further tests show your baby is healthy. If not, then you will be offered counselling to help you decide what to do.

Chorionic villus sampling (CVS) and amniocentesis (see over) check for chromosomal abnormalities, principally Down's syndrome.

These tests are usually offered only to women who have a higher risk of having a baby with a disability because there is a risk that the test may cause a miscarriage. An older mother, for example, is more likely to have a baby with Down's syndrome. A test may also be offered to a mother whose previous blood test shows a higher than normal risk.

Needle

Uterus (womb)

Placenta

Umbilical cord

Amniotic Fluid

Tube

Cervix (neck of womb)

CVS is done from about 11 weeks of pregnancy. A fine tube goes through your cervix or abdomen into the womb, and a syringe removes a sample of the chorionic villus, the tissue forming the placenta.

There is a two to four per cent risk of miscarriage, which will be discussed with you. Results take between 7 and 10 days.

Amniocentesis is done later, at between 14 and 18 weeks. The syringe takes a sample of the amniotic fluid, after a needle is inserted into the uterus, through the abdomen.

There is a one per cent risk of miscarriage, which will be discussed with you, and results can take from 10 days to a few weeks.

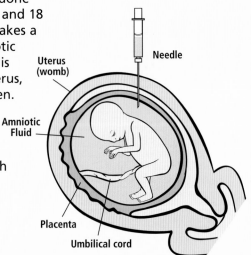

Needle

Uterus (womb)

Amniotic Fluid

Placenta

Umbilical cord

Ultrasound scanning will be used if you have CVS or amniocentesis, so that the doctor can see the exact position of the baby and the placenta. Scans are also sometimes used to detect some abnormalities. See page 44 for more information about ultrasound scanning.

Other tests you may have

In some areas, there may be a simple test to check if you are a carrier of the disease **cystic fibrosis**. This test involves giving you a mouthwash, to collect cells from the lining of your mouth. Tell the midwife or doctor if you have a family history of this condition.

You may also be offered a blood test to check for past or present infection with the **cytomegalovirus** (**CM** virus), and for **toxoplasmosis** (see page 14).

Antenatal screening and diagnosis is an area where change takes place all the time. Tests that were once offered in only a few parts of the country while their effects were being studied have become more widely available. So there may be tests on offer in your area which we haven't covered here. Before you agree to any test, you should be told how effective and reliable a test is, and if there are any side-effects.

Note: if you have Rhesus negative blood, you will be advised to have an anti-D injection after CVS and after amniocentesis.

Is there a problem?

When tests show there could be a problem, you need more information, and support.

- It's important to know what the test result shows, whether it's conclusive or not, and whether you need to make any decisions about labour or birth, or the future of your pregnancy.

- You may need time to consider your options. There are support groups that can help you with these difficult decisions (see **Further help**) and you can ask to talk with a midwife or a health visitor, as well as a doctor. If the tests indicate a disability, you may want to talk to parents who have a child with a similar condition, to get information about it. No one should try and influence you in any way; the decision has to be yours, and your partner's.

Q. I have been advised to have an amniocentesis. But I don't want to have one. Am I right?

A. Only you can decide. There is a small risk of miscarriage with amniocentesis, and you may want to compare that with the risk of having a baby with an abnormality. Discuss the comparative risks with your doctor. Or, you may not want to have a termination of pregnancy under any circumstances, and if this is the case, then there is no real reason to have an amniocentesis — though some parents want to know if their child will have a disability in order to prepare themselves for it. In any event, it is your right to decide whether or not you accept the offer of a test.

'My greatest fear was having a baby with some sort of disability, and I knew I was at a higher risk of a baby with Down's syndrome because of my age. When the amniocentesis came back and it was negative, I felt I could relax, and tell people about the pregnancy at last.'

'There is a downside to antenatal tests. My AFP test came back with a query, and I needed further investigation to rule out spina bifida. I was told there was probably nothing to worry about, but of course I did. Even when I was given the "all clear" I still worried, in case they had missed something. I think it increased my anxiety, for nothing.'

Ultrasound

SCANNING YOUR BABY DURING PREGNANCY

An ultrasound scan uses high-frequency soundwaves which bounce off solid objects. It creates a picture on a screen of your baby, the uterus, the placenta and the baby's organs. You may be offered one or more ultrasound scans.

Scans can give you and the doctor and midwife information about your baby's growth and development. They can tell you:

- your baby's size. This helps establish the dates of your pregnancy, and to ensure your baby is growing as expected
- the way your baby is lying in the uterus, which might be important at the end of pregnancy
- if twins or more are present
- the development of your baby's organs, and bones (including the spine).

They can also show:

- some abnormalities
- the exact position of the baby and placenta, to allow amniocentesis and/or CVS (see pages 41–42 for details of these procedures)

- where the placenta is lying — in late pregnancy, a low-lying placenta might cause severe bleeding, and could prevent the baby from being born vaginally (which means you'd need a Caesarean section).

When the scan is offered may differ according to local policies. For example, most units offer a scan at 16 weeks, and again later if a problem arises. If you don't wish to have any scans, or fewer than the number offered, then of course you don't have to have them.

Preparing for a scan

For a scan in early pregnancy, you'll be asked to fill your bladder first by drinking lots of water. The fullness in your bladder then pushes the uterus upwards, and this helps the radiographer get a better picture. This is a bit uncomfortable for you, as you will be dying to use the toilet for a while!

How it's done

You lie down on a flat couch, and the doctor or radiographer stands or sits next to you. You need to roll down your lower clothing, and lift up your top, so your tummy is exposed. The radiographer or doctor spreads some cold gel on your abdomen. Then a hand-held microphone-like instrument called a transducer is rolled over your abdomen. This picks up a picture of everything underneath it, and transmits it to a screen where it appears as a picture. The whole process is painless.

15 weeks

Is ultrasound safe? Most obstetricians feel there is no good evidence that ultrasound harms your baby's health or development, though it's difficult to show conclusive proof of safety. There is little evidence to show that routine scanning reduces the number of pregnancies with problems or the number of babies suffering from slow growth.

Many parents themselves report feeling reassured when a scan shows no problems. However, in the few cases where ultrasound reveals an unexpected problem, the information gained may help you and your doctors to reach a decision about whether or not to continue with the pregnancy.

questions **Q&A** answered

Q. Can the scan show whether I am having a girl or a boy?

A. Sometimes. If you want to know, just ask. You won't be told unless you want to be. You do need to bear in mind that the picture may not be clear enough, or the baby may be lying in such a way that the genitals aren't visible. The answer you get may not be the correct one.

You may not actually recognise a baby when you see the image on the screen. But the radiographer or radiologist carrying out the scan can trace the outline of your baby's body, and point out the placenta and indicate the major body organs. You will probably be able to see your baby's heart beating, and to see what position he or she is lying in. It may be possible for you to take away a photograph of the scanned image. You may be charged a small fee for this.

Q. Can my partner be with me when I have the scan?

A. Usually, yes. Or, take someone else with you if you prefer. Check before you have the scan that this is acceptable; very few places now discourage a companion.

'The first time I saw my baby on the screen was the first time I really felt pregnant — it was a wonderful moment.'

'I didn't want to have a scan. I wasn't convinced it was necessary — and though everyone just assumed I would have one, no-one criticised me for saying no.'

Your choices and how to make them

WHERE AND HOW TO HAVE YOUR BABY

Talk over the choices available with a midwife, your family doctor, your partner, with other mothers you know who have had babies in your area, and with local childbirth organisations.

The choice of places for your labour and birth are:

- **hospital, in a unit run by consultant obstetricians** (though midwives carry out most of the care). There may be more than one unit in your area. A consultant-led unit is usually chosen if you expect to need a doctor's help. Some women who have no problems still feel reassured by having specialist medical care on hand

- **hospital, in a midwife-led unit** (see page 47), if available in your area

- **domino birth**. The community midwife visits you in early labour, goes with you to hospital for the birth and returns home with you later. In some areas, there are variations on this

- **at home.** There is no evidence that a planned home birth is less safe than anywhere else for women who are not expected to have problems with pregnancy or birth. If you live in an isolated area, some way from a hospital, you may need to reconsider a decision to have a home birth.

having choices

You're usually asked to **'book' your place of birth** near the beginning of pregnancy, but you don't have to stick with your original decision though it is important that your doctor and midwife both know your plan. Once your family doctor knows you are pregnant, a midwife may come to your home to book you, or else you'll be offered an appointment at the hospital of your choice.

- Midwives are in attendance at most births — they are qualified to deal with all normal births. The doctor's role is to care for the small number of women and babies who need medical care.

- Some units in hospitals are known as **midwife-led units**, which means the midwives are responsible for running the whole unit. Generally, a midwife-led unit cares for women expecting a normal birth. For this reason, mothers expecting to need a doctor's involvement will not be encouraged to book there.

- You may be introduced to your 'named midwife' — a midwife you will see during your antenatal care and when you return home after your baby is born. In other areas, you may meet members of a team of midwives.

Independent midwives usually offer their services to women for a fee. Sometimes they charge according to your ability to pay. Increasingly, independent midwives work alongside their health service colleagues. You can still give birth at home or in hospital, as you wish. There are a few independent midwives in Scotland. For more information, see **Further help.**

'I knew the only place I would really feel comfortable and relaxed was at home. Everything's going well, and I have met most of the midwives who are likely to deliver me — that's important.'

'I prefer the idea of hospital, where there are staff and equipment immediately at hand, in case something goes wrong. We are going to visit the delivery suite, as we'd both like to know what to expect beforehand.'

Q. I would like a home birth, but I have been told home births aren't available in my area.

A. Home births may be rare in your area, but you can still choose this if you wish. You can book for a home birth with your family doctor, or with a community midwife. If you have difficulty in making these arrangements, write to the supervisor of midwives in your area about your plans to have a home birth. The supervisor should then arrange for antenatal care for you, and make sure you have midwifery care for the birth and afterwards.

WHAT SORT OF BIRTH IS RIGHT FOR YOU?

Your midwife may ask you during pregnancy if you would like to make a **birth plan.** This means that your choices are written down, after a full discussion, and after you feel you have the information on which to base your choices.

The birth plan then goes into your notes, with a copy for you to keep. Your choices are important guidelines and reminders, but you can still change your mind.

These are some of the issues you may want to consider:

● is it important for you to avoid induction or acceleration of labour? (See page 75.)

● who will be your birth companion(s)?

● do you want to use a birthing pool or bath for labour and/or birth?

● how do you want your baby's heart rate to be monitored? (See page 74.)

● do you want to be free to move into different positions during labour and delivery?

● what about pain relief? (See pages 50–51.)

● do you prefer an unaided 'physiological' third stage or an 'actively managed' third stage? (See pages 82–83.)

● are you planning to breastfeed or bottle feed? (Don't feel you have to make up your mind right away — some women aren't sure at this stage.)

● (for hospital birth) when do you think you might like to return home after the birth?

● what about Vitamin K? (See page 89.)

Water birth

Labouring in water can help you relax, and women often report that it helps with the pain of contractions. Far more women use the bath for labour than actually birth their babies in it.

You can discuss the possibility of delivering your baby in the water with the midwife or midwives who will be caring for you (if you plan a home birth) or with the antenatal clinic and the labour ward midwife (if you plan to go to hospital).

If you would like to stay in the water for a long time, it's better to use a large pool with plenty of room for you to change positions, and with room all round it. Then the midwife can examine you from all sides if necessary, and help the baby out. The water needs to be kept warm. Some hospitals have a birthing pool, or a large bath they use for labour. You can hire a special pool for use at home (see 'Pregnancy and Maternity Services' in the **Further help** section at the back of this book).

Is water birth safe? Many questions have been raised about water birth safety, and there may be concerns about cross-infection. Opinions differ amongst midwives and obstetricians — some are doubtful, others feel that with the right care, water birth is a safe option.

In the end, the choice is yours. But if you are having your baby in a hospital which has no proper facilities for water birth, or whose staff do not feel confident with water birth, you may want to think about having your baby elsewhere.

Who will be with you at the birth?

Who would you like to give you support and encouragement when you're in labour? Your partner may be the obvious choice, if you have one, but it doesn't have to be. It can be a friend.

There's some evidence that having another person with you, instead of, or as well as, your partner, is helpful, and can shorten your labour. Some women have a close friend, a relative, or their antenatal teacher. A good relationship with the professional carers is important to your whole labour — but having a companion you know already may be important, too.

PAIN RELIEF IN LABOUR

Discuss your choice of pain relief before you go into labour. Your midwife or doctor will tell you what's available. You'll be able to talk about your choices in antenatal classes, too.

You may wish to use self-help forms of pain relief or to have pain-relieving drugs of some type.

Non-chemical pain relief

Most antenatal classes teach breathing awareness, as a way of coping with the pain of contractions. The emphasis is on breathing as a way of relaxation, which helps you cope with the pain.

Relaxation doesn't take away pain, but it can prevent pain becoming stronger, because tension increases pain levels. The main aim is to help you to be able to cope with the pain and not be overwhelmed by it. Then you will be fully conscious, and in as much control of your labour as you want to be. There is research to show that when women are relaxed, they release the body's own hormone-like pain-relievers — endorphins.

It is important to some women to avoid drugs in labour, as all drug-based methods have some disadvantages to mother or baby or both. You may want to rely on yourself, with the support and encouragement of those around you. There are no disadvantages to breathing and relaxation, but sometimes they may not work if your labour is long, complicated, or just too painful for you.

Other non-drug pain relief includes hypnosis, acupuncture and acupressure. You need to see a practitioner in these methods first. Lying in water can also help (see page 49), as can massage.

TENS — **stands for Transcutaneous Electrical Nerve Stimulation.** It is a form of pain relief provided by a small box wired to electrodes which fix on your skin, and which give out a slight electrical charge. It can be effective in relieving pain, and it is safe for you and your baby. If you want to use this, ask the hospital if you can hire or borrow a TENS machine so that you can start to use it as soon as labour begins.

Entonox — sometimes known as 'laughing gas', or 'gas and air'. This is the brand name for the mix of 50 per cent nitrous oxide, and 50 per cent oxygen. The gas comes in a cylinder, attached to a tube and a mask which you place on your face. There may be a mouthpiece you can use instead. At the start of a contraction, begin taking deep breaths of gas.

Effects: the effects start about 15 or 20 seconds after you first breathe it in. If it works for you, it takes the 'edge' off the peak of the pain and this relief lasts until the end of the contraction. You can't overdose on Entonox. This is because you become drowsy as you use it, and your hand holding the mask or mouthpiece just falls away as you drop off, preventing you from breathing in any more. Your body also expels this gas quickly.

Babies appear not to be affected; very little Entonox reaches them.

Pethidine — one of a number of drugs related to morphine which are given in labour. Other common forms include diamorphine. It is injected, usually in the buttocks, in varying doses.

Effects: pethidine takes about 15 minutes to work. Its effects last a couple of hours, depending on the strength of the dose. It can make you feel a bit 'out of it', as if the pain is there but you're not experiencing it. Some

women feel this distancing effect as 'being out of control'. Others like it and find it allows them to doze between contractions. Some women feel sick after pethidine, so an anti-sickness medicine is usually given at the same time.

Pethidine can affect the baby's breathing at birth. The baby may be sleepier and less interested in feeding for two or three days afterwards. If your baby's breathing is poor as a result of pethidine a drug can be given to treat this. The effect on breathing is more likely if pethidine is given within two or three hours before birth, and you may be advised not to have it for this reason. If pethidine is given four or more hours before birth, the effects have a better chance to wear off in the mother. The effects will remain in the baby for longer, say up to 48 hours, after birth.

Epidural anaesthesia — an anaesthetic drug is injected into the epidural space at the side of the spinal cord. You may be asked to curl up on your side while the anaesthetist inserts the epidural, or you may be able to sit up, leaning forward over a pillow. A fine plastic tube — a catheter — is left in so that more anaesthetic can be given if needed. You're usually given a drip to help maintain normal blood pressure (low blood pressure can be a side-effect).

Effects: total pain relief for most women (although for a few they may only get relief down one side). You may have no feeling at all in the lower half of your body, which may make it harder for you to push in second stage. This numbness will last for some hours. Some maternity units offer mobile epidurals, which enable some feeling to remain in your lower limbs so you can stand or walk or change position.

Just occasionally, you may have a bad headache for some days after the birth, and some mothers may get backache.

Forceps delivery may be more common because you can lose the urge to push. On the other hand, some doctors feel that having an epidural, especially for a long labour might increase the chances of a vaginal delivery, as the pain relief and relaxation some women experience with it allows labour to progress.

Are all forms of pain relief always available?

At home, the midwife can give you Entonox, and/or pethidine. In hospital you usually have all forms available, although in some units epidurals may not be available round the clock as there may be no anaesthetist there.

Drink lots of water as dehydration can be a major cause of discomfort.

Changes to your body

MINOR PROBLEMS

Most women will experience some of these very common 'side-effects' of pregnancy — but you'd be very unlucky to have them all!

If you have persistent problems, see your doctor or you may like to try alternative remedies as prescribed by an expert.

FOOD CRAVINGS — very common at any stage in pregnancy. You may want odd food combinations, or get a liking for large quantities of something you haven't enjoyed before. As long as you continue to eat a healthy diet (see page 13) you don't need to worry.

HEARTBURN (INDIGESTION) — a burning sensation round the breastbone, caused by stomach juices and foods. It's more common in later pregnancy. Eat small amounts of food more often if you are affected by this. Take your time when you eat. Strong tea/coffee, pure fruit juice, spicy and fatty foods can cause heartburn.

CONSTIPATION — this is very common in pregnancy. Eat more fresh fruit and vegetables and more wholegrain breads and cereals, to increase your fibre intake. Drink more — a glass of water with every meal and in between.

THRUSH — a thick white vaginal discharge, accompanied by itching and soreness, also known as candidiasis. Your doctor can prescribe vaginal pessaries, tested as safe to use in pregnancy.

PASSING URINE OFTEN — this is normal, and caused by pregnancy hormones and the increasing compression of your bladder.

Occasionally, there may be a urine infection. Mention it your midwife.

STRESS INCONTINENCE — the bladder leaks a little urine. This happens because the pelvic floor muscles are put under stress when you cough, sneeze or run. It happens especially in later pregnancy. Pelvic floor exercises (see page 92) can help to strengthen the muscles. If necessary, wear a pad to keep you comfortable. Continue to do your exercises after the birth.

CYSTITIS — a urine infection causing a burning sensation on passing urine, and the feeling of needing to pass urine all the time. If persistent your doctor can treat this. Try drinking lots of water to help flush out the infection.

VARICOSE VEINS — swollen veins, usually in the legs but sometimes in the vulva (vaginal opening), too. They may cause aching and sometimes itching. Support tights or stockings can help. Don't stand for long periods, and rest with your legs up when you can. Always tell your midwife or doctor if you notice any hot, red or painful areas in your legs.

PILES OR HAEMORRHOIDS — these are varicose veins of the back passage, or anus. They are sometimes painful and itchy, and they can be made worse by constipation. Your doctor can treat them.

BACKACHE — flat shoes or shoes with a low heel will help. Sit and stand with your back straight, and shoulders dropped. Be careful about lifting heavy weights — always bend at the knees to do so. There are some specific exercises that can help — ask your midwife, obstetric physiotherapist or antenatal teacher.

SWELLING OF THE ANKLES, FINGERS, FACE AND HANDS, or oedema, happens because the body holds more fluid in pregnancy. A certain amount of oedema is normal in later pregnancy, but more severe cases can indicate pre-eclampsia, if present with other signs (see pages 55–56).

Sometimes fluid collects in the wrists and produces a painful or tingling sensation in the fingers. This is called 'carpal tunnel syndrome'. Raising your hands above your head for several minutes may help to drain the fluid away. If it is very troublesome, speak to your midwife or GP. They can refer you to an obstetric physiotherapist who may give you lightweight splints to wear on your wrists. The condition usually goes away after the birth.

Don't keep your worries to yourself. Most pregnancy problems aren't serious for you or your baby's health (although they may not seem so at the time). Your midwife or doctor will give you advice and reassurance about how to deal with most of the less serious discomforts of pregnancy.

If you need to talk to a midwife, call the antenatal clinic at the hospital where you plan to give birth. If you know someone by name, ask for that person. Or you can telephone your community midwife.

HOW MUCH WEIGHT IS GAINED IN PREGNANCY?

You can expect to gain between 9 and 16 kg (19 and 35 pounds) in weight during your pregnancy. The average is about 12.5 kg (28 pounds).

Your weight gain is made up like this:

- baby 2.5–4 kg (5–9 pounds)
- placenta 500–1000 g (1–2 pounds)
- amniotic fluid 1.5–2.5 kg (3–5 pounds)
- extra weight of uterus, breasts and energy stores of fat 2–5 kg (4–11 pounds)
- extra weight of blood 2–4 kg (4–9 pounds).

You may gain weight from the very start of pregnancy, mainly because of extra fluid and fluid retention. Many women put on very little in the last two to three weeks, or stop gaining altogether.

You'll be weighed at the start of the pregnancy, for future comparisons, but you may not be weighed at every antenatal appointment. This is because the information gained is not always useful, and weighing can make some women unnecessarily anxious.

More serious problems

IS THERE SOMETHING WRONG?

You may need treatment, or careful observation, if there are signs of more serious problems in your pregnancy. These problems include:

Anaemia

This means you are lacking in iron, and/or folic acid, and/or Vitamin B12. The condition shows up in a blood test. Anaemia may be a result of illness, poor diet, severe sickness, or extra strain on your body such as when you are expecting twins. You will be given information on changing your diet, and you may be prescribed iron supplements.

Bleeding

You should get medical advice straight away if you notice you are bleeding from the vagina in pregnancy, or if you experience severe, abdominal pain. Sometimes, the placenta is lying so low it covers the cervix. It is more likely to bleed in this position. This condition — placenta

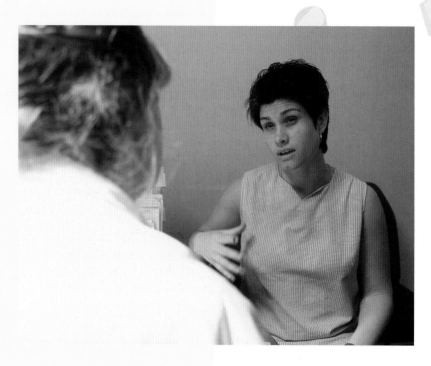

praevia — is uncommon and needs careful observation. Any bleeding from the vagina in pregnancy should be taken seriously. In later pregnancy it could be that the placenta is separating from the uterine wall. This could be life-threatening to you and your baby.

Not all instances of bleeding are serious — some women do bleed a little on and off all the way through pregnancy, for a variety of minor reasons.

Continued sickness

If you are unfortunate, the pregnancy sickness that usually goes at around 12

weeks persists into later pregnancy. Very severe cases, known as hyperemesis gravidarum, need hospital treatment.

Diabetes

Some women develop diabetes during pregnancy. The condition disappears after pregnancy, though some women do go on to develop diabetes later. The pregnancy may be affected, as the baby tends to get larger, and the diabetes will be monitored to make sure it remains under control.

High blood pressure

When blood pressure is very high it can be diagnosed as pregnancy-induced hypertension. If it's present with other symptoms it can be a sign of pre-eclampsia (see pages 55–56). High blood pressure can affect the placenta.

Itching

Occasionally women develop a severe itching of the skin in pregnancy. This is usually no more than a highly irritating discomfort — but occasionally it can be the sign of a condition called obstetric cholestasis, which can affect the liver. See your doctor or midwife if your itch doesn't clear up, or if no treatment helps.

OTHER PROBLEMS

Separated symphysis pubis

This happens when the small joint (the symphysis pubis) at the front of the bony girdle of the pelvis opens up too far. It can happen in pregnancy or at birth. It can cause a lot of pain on walking or even standing. Physiotherapy can help, or a support belt worn across the pelvis to keep the joint together while it gets back to its normal pre-pregnancy state. (See also **Further help** at the back of this book.)

Separation of the long abdominal muscles

When this happens, the uterus needs extra support as the pregnancy progresses.

PRE-ECLAMPSIA

This condition occurs only in pregnancy, and affects one in every 10 pregnancies. Most cases are mild, but some (about 1 first pregnancy in every 100) are dangerous for the baby and the mother.

When a mother has severe pre-eclampsia or eclampsia, her labour may be induced, even though this might mean a pre-term delivery. Other babies are born early because the mother has pre-eclampsia, and she goes into pre-term labour anyway, without induction.

The condition is 'pre' (before)-eclampsia, because if it is not treated, or treated too late, it can develop into eclampsia. Eclampsia is always very dangerous, but fortunately very rare. The signs of pre-eclampsia are:

- consistently high blood pressure in late pregnancy (after 20 weeks, and especially after 30 weeks)
- severe oedema (swelling), due to fluid retention, in the ankles, fingers, face
- headaches/visual disturbances
- protein present in the urine
- poor growth in the baby.

'Do I have to go into hospital?'

Today, some conditions are observed and treated at home, perhaps by the GP or the community midwife. Sometimes, you can go into hospital for daycare only, returning home at night.

However, if you are at risk of bleeding, or of going into pre-term labour, hospital may be the best place for you, especially if your home is some distance away and you cannot get to hospital quickly in an emergency. Sometimes, pregnant women go into hospital because of severe sickness, or because they have a condition that needs to be watched.

Routine antenatal checking of your blood pressure and your urine in pregnancy is mainly to detect the development of pre-eclampsia.

The cause of pre-eclampsia and/or high blood pressure is not fully understood, and the links between the main signs are still very unclear. At least two of the main signs must be present before pre-eclampsia is diagnosed.

Note: In very serious cases of pre-eclampsia, the mother may feel very unwell. She may vomit, and have a very bad headache, visual disturbances and severe pain in and around the abdomen. She needs hospital treatment immediately. These could all be signs of developing eclampsia which is characterised by convulsions. Always report these symptoms to the midwife or doctor.

For more information contact APEC (Action on Pre-eclampsia). Details can be found in the **Further help** section.

Q. My baby isn't growing very well. Is this serious?

A. It may be, but some babies are naturally small, and some catch up in later pregnancy. Your dates may be incorrect, so you may not be as far on in your pregnancy as you think. Most babies are born healthy. It's very difficult to diagnose accurately if a baby isn't growing well. Most women who are told they have small babies give birth to normal, healthy babies.

Some babies have intrauterine growth retardation (IUGR), which means they are smaller and lighter than most healthy babies at this stage of pregnancy. IUGR may happen because the placenta isn't nourishing the baby well, or perhaps because the baby has an underlying condition which is preventing growth. If the mother's diet is very poor, this can cause poor growth in the baby. Smoking also causes the baby to be less well-nourished, and therefore smaller. Occasionally, poor growth in the baby can be a sign of pre-eclampsia in the mother.

Very small babies are at a greater risk of pre-term birth and its hazards. They may have development problems that go on into childhood. Sometimes, the baby has a better chance of growing and surviving outside the uterus, and the doctor may advise you that the best option is to induce labour (see page 67).

If your baby isn't growing well, further investigations will be discussed with you. You may have more scans, for example, so that your baby's development can be measured more accurately.

Pregnancy & work

YOUR RIGHTS AND BENEFITS

You need to make decisions regarding your job. When can you leave before your baby's born? Do you plan to return after your baby, and if so, when?

Maternity leave

You must tell your employer you are pregnant not later than 21 days before you take maternity leave (though many women prefer to do this earlier, of course). You are entitled to 14 weeks maternity leave, however many hours you work, and however long you have been employed.

The earliest you can start your leave is 11 weeks before the expected week of the birth.

If you have worked for the same employer for two years by the end of the 12th week before your baby is due, you are eligible for extended maternity leave — that is, you can return to your employment up to 29 weeks after the week in which the baby is born, on top of the 11 weeks you have taken before the birth.

Your job is protected. It is illegal for your employer to dismiss you or make you redundant for any reason connected with your pregnancy, the birth, or your maternity leave. This applies no matter how many hours you work, and no matter how long you have worked for the same employer.

Some jobs and some workplaces may have agreed maternity rights that are better and more flexible than the ones laid down in law. You should always check with your contract of employment, your personnel department, or your trade union representative, to make sure of what you are entitled to.

Maternity benefits and payments

Working out the money that's due to you during and after pregnancy is quite complicated.

Statutory Maternity Pay (SMP)

When you are 26 weeks pregnant your midwife or GP can give you form MAT B1, which is the maternity certificate, 'proving' you are pregnant. You send this to your employer at least 21 days before you intend to stop work, together with the date you plan to go on leave. Your employer will arrange for you to get SMP.

SMP is a weekly payment made to you by your employer (who then claims most of it back from the Benefits Agency).
You get it:

● if you have worked for the same employer for at least 26 weeks by the end of the 15th week before your baby is due

● if you earn up to a minimum amount each week.

For the up-to-date figures, check with your employer, your union, or your Citizens' Advice Bureau. SMP is payable for up to 18 weeks, but if you are only entitled to 14 weeks maternity leave, you will only get 14 weeks SMP.

The amount is 90 per cent of your average weekly pay, and then a basic rate after this (the basic rate is liable to change).

When to leave, when to return?

These decisions are up to you. You can work right up to the day your baby is born if you wish, and you will still be entitled to the same amount of leave from your job — it just means it will all be taken after the birth instead of before.

Maternity Allowance

This is a payment for women who can't get SMP (the self-employed, or women who have given up work or changed jobs during the pregnancy). It is paid for up to 18 weeks. Women applying for Maternity Allowance must have worked and paid full-rate National Insurance contributions for at least 26 of the 66 weeks before the expected week of the birth.

To claim Maternity Allowance, get form MA1 from your antenatal clinic or from your local Benefits Agency, and send it with the certificate MATB1, from your GP or midwife, to the Benefits Agency, as soon as you can after 26 weeks of pregnancy.

Child Benefit and One Parent Benefit

These benefits are payable from the date the baby is born. They come from the Benefits Agency. There is a form for Child Benefit on the back of their leaflet *Babies and Benefits*. You need form CH11 if you want to claim One Parent Benefit. Send the completed forms with your baby's birth certificate in the pre-paid envelope.

Maternity Payment from the Social Fund

This is a lump sum grant for expectant mothers on Income Support, means-tested JobSeeker's Allowance, Family Credit or Disability Working Allowance. The Benefits Agency also has form SF100 for claims. Send it back with your MATB1 at any time from 11 weeks before the birth. If you send it after the birth, do it within three months, and send it with a copy of the baby's birth certificate instead of the MATB1.

> Your local Benefits Agency office can help you with more information. Also, see **Further help** at the back of this book.

WORKING AFTER YOUR BABY'S BORN

It's not easy being a working parent, no matter what age your child is when you decide to start work outside the home, or return to work. Finding high-quality childcare is important, of course, and if you plan on returning after a few months, you may want to look at your options while you are still pregnant.

- Anyone offering daycare to babies and young children should be registered with your local authority, including workplace nurseries or crèches. This ensures safety checks have been made, and that there is a correct ratio of staff to children. You can get a list of registered minders, nurseries and crèches in your area. Ask other parents about their experiences, and visit the minder or the nursery, with or without your child, as many times as you need to feel confident.

- When the day comes to leave your child, you are bound to have anxieties. It will help if you get your child used to the new carer or carers before you have to leave. But it can be an emotional time, and many parents feel pressures at being split from their work and from their need to be with their child. There are no easy answers to this — having more flexible and responsive workplaces would help in matching the needs of parents with small children and work.

Twins

WILL PREGNANCY AND BIRTH BE DIFFERENT?

Twins (and more) are formed either by the egg splitting shortly after fertilisation (identical twins), or by two or more eggs being fertilised by two or more sperm (non-identical or fraternal twins). Non-identical twins are slightly more likely to happen after a course of fertility treatment which stimulates ovulation, and which means more than one egg may be released. They can also happen when more than one fertilised egg is put into the uterus after in-vitro fertilisation (test-tube pregnancy).

Twins may show up on the screen during an ultrasound scan. They may be suspected because your uterus is larger than expected at this stage of pregnancy.

The main concern of a multiple pregnancy, even if you are healthy and have no major problems, is that you may get double helpings of the minor discomforts of pregnancy. That means (for

example) more backache, fatigue, heartburn and nausea, constipation and piles. The increased weight gain, and the excess of pregnancy hormones, contribute to this. Try to rest, especially later on in pregnancy. A healthy diet is particularly important.

Extra care

If you are expecting twins, or more, you will receive more attention during pregnancy.

The reasons for this extra care include:

- greater chance of high blood pressure, which needs careful observation, and possible treatment

- twins or more are likely to be born before 40 weeks — 37 or 38 weeks is average for twins, but 25 per cent of twin pregnancies end before 36 weeks

- birth problems are more common, and Caesarean section may be necessary to speed up delivery, or to deliver the second twin quickly. Less space in the uterus means one or both twins may be in a difficult, or impossible, position for a vaginal birth.

Triplet pregnancy is even more likely than twins to end in a pre-term, and/or operative delivery. Caesarean section is considered virtually inevitable for quads or quints, to speed up and control the delivery. Even so, while multiple pregnancy is hard work, and a multiple labour and delivery may be more of a challenge to everyone, especially you, the majority of twin and triplet births are as joyous and rewarding as any other, and many pregnancies and births are perfectly straightforward.

Q. Is it possible to breastfeed twins?

A. Yes. Your body is capable of making as much milk as your babies need. Twins double the demand on the breast milk production, and therefore they double the supply. It is equally possible to breastfeed triplets (and more!).

The practicalities, however, of feeding more than one baby are something of a challenge. The babies may be small and they may tire easily, so you may have to work quite hard at first in getting them interested in feeding. You may need skilled help to teach them to latch on well (see page 99). You'll need time to decide which is the best way of feeding — two together or separately. Even when you think you have got it sorted out, you may find you have to change to suit your babies' changing needs.

Twins tend to differ in their feeding habits, just as any other two babies might, and keeping them both happy may be hard in the early weeks. You need to feel confident, and to have encouragement from the people around you. You also need help with any other jobs in the house. In time, feeding becomes less intensive — and many women find it easier than making up bottles of formula milk.

MULTIPLE BIRTHS — THE STATISTICS

The birth of more than one baby is always known as a multiple birth, whether there are two, three or more. One baby at a time is known as a singleton.

- 1 pregnancy in every 80 is a twin pregnancy.

- 1 pregnancy in 8000 is triplets.

- 1 pregnancy in 800,000 is quads.

Multiple pregnancy tends to run in families, down the female line. The tendency to release more than one egg at ovulation seems to be inherited. The twins which 'run in families' are non-identical, because of this.

Twins in the uterus — how do they lie?

The best presentation of twins is both head-down — 'cephalic' or 'vertex' — and is the most common. However, pressure of space in the uterus means it's also not uncommon for one or both babies to be breech (feet or bottom down). Transverse lie (baby across the uterus) is also a possibility, and if this is the case with the first presenting twin, a Caesarean section is inevitable. If the second twin is lying across, there may be an attempt to turn the second twin, after the first twin has been born vaginally.

In touch with your baby

YOUR BABY'S 'EXPERIENCES'

It's known that unborn babies have some awareness of their surroundings, and may be able to respond to them.

Over the years, researchers have tried to study the responses of the unborn baby. It is possible to study some physical reactions to certain happenings.

A memory of the uterus?

Parents and unborn babies have been studied together and followed up after the birth. This work points to the possibility that babies have some sort of memory of their life in the womb.

In one study, some pregnant mothers had the habit of relaxing with a cup of tea and a well-known soap opera on the television, each afternoon in late pregnancy. After they were born, their babies were found to relax whenever the researchers played them the soap's signature tune.

Your baby can dream — maybe

The nerve pathways of the brain are as developed in a baby of just 28 weeks gestation as they are in a baby at term. From week 32, tests can detect REM (rapid eye movement) sleep in a baby. In adults, REM sleep means the person is dreaming. Researchers think that the unborn baby may be reliving, by this dreaming, some of the experiences of moving, of hearing, of seeing and feeling, in preparation for life outside the womb.

What you can do

● Play music regularly to your baby — perhaps set aside a time, say 10 minutes a few times a week, for this. The research shows that unborn babies are more restful, as if listening, when simple melodies are played.

● You and your partner can talk to your baby, while lying down and relaxing. Your baby can hear your voice, and can get to know it better when it's not competing with other noises. It doesn't matter what you say, but use a calm, regular tone of voice. Try reciting nursery rhymes if you don't know what to say.

● The fetus is sensitive to touch from very early on in the pregnancy. In the second half of pregnancy, you can feel clear movements. You can touch and massage your abdomen — gently and regularly. You can use a vegetable oil such as almond oil, or a light moisturising cream, to make it more pleasant for you. Your partner can share in the massage.

'I used to talk to our baby when I was on my own. It just felt natural to me, to have a little chat from time to time. I would tell him how much we were looking forward to him coming to be with us, and what we'd do together. I found it was very relaxing, and calming, for me to do this.'

Antenatal classes

WHAT'S ON OFFER, HOW TO CHOOSE?

About half of all pregnant women attend some antenatal or preparation for parenthood classes. A typical class will form part of a course of six to eight, which you'd go to towards the end of your pregnancy. There are many variations. Some classes are open and 'rolling' — you can join at any time and leave at any time. Some classes are specially designed for different groups of mothers — teenage mothers, for example, or mothers from the same ethnic background.

Antenatal classes cover a wide range of topics, but in most you can expect to hear about:

- health in pregnancy, with advice on diet and coping with minor discomforts

- what to expect in later pregnancy, and in labour and birth
- pain relief options
- coping with labour and birth using self-help techniques such as relaxation and breathing
- possible problems with labour and birth
- Caesarean section, forceps, ventouse delivery
- exercises for pregnancy, birth and afterwards
- baby feeding

- caring for your baby in the early days and weeks
- birth plans.

Most clinics, hospitals and health centres have antenatal classes. They are free, and are usually run by midwives and/or health visitors. Other non-NHS classes may charge a fee. They're run by specially-trained antenatal teachers, who may also be, but usually are not, health professionals. They are almost always mothers themselves. NHS classes are usually held in a room in the clinic itself — other classes may be in the teacher's own home.

questions & answered

Q. How do I find out what's available to me locally?

A. Your midwife or health visitor is a good source of information. Any health professional can find out where the local clinic or hospital classes are, and their times and dates. For information about National Childbirth Trust classes, and classes run by members of the Scottish Birth Teachers Association, or others, see the addresses at the back of this book, or try your local telephone book.

Q. What about payment for non-NHS classes?

A. Fees for non-NHS classes vary, but on the whole, teachers don't like to feel that women might be put off from coming because they can't afford the fees. There are often subsidised class fees, or paying by easy instalments. In some cases, fees may not be charged at all. Just ask at the time of booking.

A good antenatal class will be much more than someone standing at the front talking to you. It will:

● encourage you to ask about, and discuss, things that are important to you

● explain everything in a way you understand

● help you face labour, birth and early parenthood with confidence.

It will offer support and encouragement in a warm, friendly atmosphere so you can make new friends and feel the rest of the class is supporting you, too.

Choosing the right class is easier if you ask around first. The midwife will know about classes, and which ones have good reports. If you know mothers who have given birth recently, ask them if they went to any good classes. You can go to more than one set of classes, if you wish.

Your partner at antenatal classes

Some antenatal classes are run for couples and while they may be happy to have mothers only along, too, you may feel a little uncomfortable if you are the only one on your own. Consider taking a friend along instead.

Some antenatal courses have a couples session or 'men only' sessions.

It's up to you and your partner, if you have one, to decide what's right for you. Some partners are quite adamant they don't want to go to any of the classes, and some mothers-to-be prefer to be on their own. Sharing in an antenatal class is a good way for partners to meet others who may have similar concerns, and it gives them a chance to ask questions, too. Partners can find out how to support you at the birth, and during breastfeeding. You can practise massage and relaxation techniques, and make new friends as a couple.

If your partner is a woman, your relationship can be kept confidential, or not, just as you prefer. Female friends and relatives often accompany women to classes.

Preparing for your baby

WHAT YOU BOTH NEED

You don't have to buy everything your baby needs in one go. Lots of baby equipment isn't needed until much later. Babies need clothes, nappies, somewhere warm and clean to sleep, something to 'ride' in like a baby carrier, pram or pushchair (with a lie-back position), bedding, a car safety seat if you use a car — and that's it for the first few months.

Bottle-fed babies will need bottles and sterilising equipment (see page 108).

Optional extras in the very early weeks

- Baby carrier or sling.

- Baby bath — useful but not essential. Your baby can use the big bath, or even a clean washing-up bowl in the first week or two.

- Crib/Moses basket — pretty and more portable than the 'big' cot, but soon outgrown.

- Cuddly toys — attractive in the baby's room, but of no interest to your baby for the first months.

- Changing mat or table — any clean, covered flat surface, including the floor, or your lap, can be used for your baby's nappy changes (if you have had a Caesarean section, you'll need a raised surface, such as a mat on top of a changing unit or dressing table).

- Breast pump — you won't need this straight away, and in any case, hand expressing of breast milk, without using a pump, is a useful skill to learn (see page 106).

For some suggestions about the clothing your baby will need, see page 113.

You can save money if you:

- buy second hand where possible. Check equipment for stability and safety (see also page 114)

- use hand-me-downs — good baby clothing can be used for several babies

- don't buy newborn-sized baby clothes. The next size up may look big, but your baby doesn't care. (Small or pre-term babies will need some newborn clothing, though.)

- cut down old bed sheets and hem them for cot and pram bedding

- borrow equipment which you'll need for no more than a few weeks or months, or share the cost with a friend or relative whose baby is due some months before or after yours.

Pre-term labour

WHEN YOUR BABY ARRIVES EARLY

Pre-term labour is generally defined as labour beginning before the 37th week of pregnancy. Over the last few years, babies born early have had a greater chance of surviving and developing without any long-term problems. The outlook for a pre-term baby is affected by:

● the number of weeks you are pregnant (the later, the better)

● the baby's size. Bigger babies usually have a better chance of survival, as long as they are healthy in other ways

● whether the baby has any birth abnormality

● the availability of specialist care.

It is very rare for any baby to survive more than a short time if born before 23 weeks. At 24 weeks, just under half of all babies survive. A baby born at 25 weeks has a slightly higher than 50 per cent chance of survival. At 26 weeks, 75 per cent, and at 28 weeks, 85 per cent of babies survive. By the time the pregnancy has reached the 35th week, the baby is likely to be fine, but may have to spend some time in special care. Some pre-term babies survive but have a permanent or long-term disability or health problem.

Why are some babies born early?

It's not always known why some women go into labour early. There are several possible reasons:

● infection in the mother

● conditions such as pre-eclampsia

● more than one baby. Most twins and triplets are born before 38 weeks, and many sooner than this. The uterus starts to contract when it is over-stretched

● weakness in the cervix.

If your labour starts early, you will either experience rupture of the membranes (your waters will 'break'), or you will start to feel contractions. If you suspect you are in labour, or if you are bleeding, call the hospital straight away.

It may be possible to slow down or even stop your labour. Drugs that stop you contracting may give your baby more time in the uterus. You may also be given treatment to prevent your baby being born with respiratory distress syndrome, a condition which seriously affects breathing.

Occasionally, a mother might be advised she needs to have her labour induced because she has a condition that threatens her health, or her baby's health. Or, her baby might be thought to have a better chance of health or survival outside the uterus (see page 75 for more information on induction).

For information about your baby in special care, see page 29.

When pregnancy goes wrong

LOSING YOUR BABY BEFORE BIRTH

As many as one in four pregnancies miscarry, though the usual figure given is about one in six confirmed pregnancies. A miscarriage is defined as the loss of the fetus before 24 weeks. About one baby in every 200 is stillborn (dies in the uterus after 24 weeks).

Some pregnancies end after termination for abnormality.

Miscarriage

The medical term for a miscarriage is a 'spontaneous abortion'. Most miscarriages happen in the first three months, and most miscarriages have no clear cause. We know that early miscarriages — before 12 weeks of pregnancy — are usually the result of a 'blighted ovum' when the pregnancy does not develop correctly, for no apparent reason.

Sometimes, the pregnancy has ended, but the embryo remains in the uterus. This is called a missed abortion. In time it would be expelled without any intervention, although a short minor operation called an 'evacuation of uterus' is often offered. This would be done under an anaesthetic.

Occasionally, miscarriages are caused by a condition called cervical incompetence. This means that the cervix doesn't stay closed. It starts to dilate, while the uterus contracts. The baby is lost before about the 20th week.

Ectopic pregnancy

The pregnancy has developed outside the uterus, usually in the fallopian tube (see page 17).

Hydatidiform mole

This is not a true pregnancy, but a collection of fluid-filled sacs growing from the tissue that would have become the placenta. The mole is removed by an operation, or by inducing the uterus to expel it.

Stillbirth

Some babies die in the uterus, or very shortly after birth (when the death will be recorded as a peri-natal death). This could be because of a serious abnormality. Or the placenta may have stopped functioning well, and the baby lacks oxygen as a result. Often, it's just not known why the baby dies.

Saying goodbye to your baby

With later miscarriage, and stillbirth, you will give birth to your baby, after a labour and delivery. Many parents find it helpful to hold their baby, when possible. This acknowledges the depth of grief at the loss of a real little person, who was wanted and who would have been welcomed with love. You can dress or wrap your baby and care for him or her tenderly. A midwife or doctor can take a picture for you. You may not want to hold your baby straight away, but a sensitive midwife will ask you once or twice if you want to — so many parents later treasure the memory that she will want to make sure you have the chance to say yes.

Ask the hospital what arrangements can be made for a funeral, or you can arrange your own. The hospital chaplain can be a good source of support and information, whether or not you are religious.

Your midwife or doctor may ask your permission to carry out a post-mortem examination on your baby. This may help give information about why your baby died. A post-mortem is always done sensitively, and you will hardly notice any effects of it.

Q. I have had two early miscarriages, and I have been told just to try again. How can I make sure I don't lose another baby, if I get pregnant again?

A. The usual medical definition of 'recurrent miscarriage' is when three or more miscarriages have happened in succession. Having two miscarriages is very distressing for you, but it's probably nothing to do with any underlying condition. You have a very high chance of carrying your next pregnancy to term. However, you will need emotional support, as the next pregnancy is likely to be an anxious time for you.

Emotional support after pregnancy loss

Other women who have lost babies may be a great support for you. Just knowing you are not alone can mean a great deal. With other people who understand, you don't have to pretend to be brave. See **Further help** at the back of this book for the addresses and phone numbers of groups who can help.

Your midwife, and your GP, can offer you support, and should be able to go through your notes with you, to help you under-stand, if it's possible, why you lost your baby, and reassure you that you are in no way to blame. After a late miscarriage or a stillbirth, you will need midwifery care, to make sure your body is recovering from the pregnancy.

People may tend to think about the mother most after a miscarriage or a stillbirth, but partners need support, too. Your partner may also be the main link between you and the health professionals, which can be very stressful.

'I felt I was the only one to have lost a baby — I'd hardly heard the word "stillbirth" before in my life. Then, when I met people, they didn't seem to know what to say to me. I could see people crossing the road rather than talk to me. I felt so alone. I suppose they were too embarrassed — but it felt like they just didn't care. Or they cared more about their own embarrassment than my pain.'

BECOMING PREGNANT AGAIN

If you have recently lost a baby, you may not want to think about becoming pregnant again for a while, if ever; or you may yearn to fill the empty space in your arms, and your life, with another baby. People's feelings differ. There's no 'right' or 'normal' way to feel.

There's no 'right' time to become pregnant again, either. Medically, about three to six months is the time needed to allow your body to recover and to establish a menstrual cycle. But emotionally, this may be too soon for you. Only you know what's right — some couples want to leave space to allow for grieving. It can be hard to look forward to a new birth when you are still so sad about the baby you lost.

WILL IT HAPPEN AGAIN?

Most causes of stillbirths, neonatal deaths and miscarriages are unlikely to recur. But there are a few causes which could recur, and you will be offered information on what to expect.

Sometimes, pre-conception care or genetic counselling can help next time, especially if you are concerned that either you or your partner may have a health problem or an inherited condition that could affect pregnancy. Your doctor can refer you to a specialist in this sort of care.

Labour

WHAT TO LOOK OUT FOR

Your labour and birth are unique and women's experiences vary — all normal, but none predictable. The beginning of labour is often not clear-cut, and sometimes it can start without you being fully aware of it. The first signs of labour can happen within a few hours of each other, or they could be spread out over a longer period of time. The obvious signs are:

- **the 'show':** this is the release of the mucus plug, or operculum, which seals the opening of the cervix. In some women it comes out of the vagina as a single blob of pinkish jelly; in others it is a series of smaller pieces, and in others it can be reddish brown and blood-tinged. It is a sign that the cervix is beginning to stretch and soften a little, in preparation for labour. It may not mean you are actually in labour. It can be several days between the show and the start of labour proper, or just an hour or so, or anything in between

- **'breaking of the waters':** the membranes, or amniotic sac, is the bag of fluid surrounding the baby inside the uterus. When the membranes break, or rupture, the fluid escapes. It can happen as a sudden gush of liquid down your legs. More usually, though, it will start to trickle. Telephone your doctor, midwife or the hospital if your waters break. There may be a risk of infection to the baby if the membranes rupture and labour doesn't start within a day or so. If the baby's head is not yet engaged, or if your baby is breech, a rush of waters may bring the cord with it. The cord could then become compressed, which would be risky for your baby's oxygen supply

● **contractions:** these are the only sure signs of labour if they gradually come closer together and last longer than 40 seconds. You should feel them getting stronger, longer and more rhythmical, too.

If you're not sure what to do, contact the maternity unit where you plan to give birth, or your community midwife. Describe your symptoms, and you will be advised on whether you need to do anything other than wait and see what happens over the next few hours. You may have a visit from a midwife, whether or not you plan a home birth, who can examine you if necessary, and help you decide where the best place is for you.

WHAT IS A CONTRACTION?

The uterus is a network of muscle fibres, and contractions happen when the fibres shorten. They do this to pull up the cervix and to press down at the top of the uterus. The muscles relax as the contraction dies away. With each contraction the muscles stay shorter than they were. This leaves the cervix slightly more open and pushes the baby a little further down.

Contractions usually feel like a tightening sensation across your tummy and possibly into your back and thighs. They usually begin gently, build up to a peak and then trail off. They may remind you of period pains (which are also contractions of the uterus), or feel much more painful. Women have different experiences with contractions, as the intensity can vary a lot.

Sometimes women can start to have contractions only for them to fade away. This can be deceptive, and many women think they are in labour. They go to hospital, only to find everything stops. If this happens to you, you may be examined, and you may be disappointed that you are not very far on in your labour; maybe your cervix doesn't show that the contractions have had any effect at all.

In this situation, you may be asked if you'd prefer to go home. This is sensible, unless you live a long way from the hospital. Don't feel embarrassed. This sort of false alarm happens all the time.

SEX AND LABOUR

There is a widespread idea that sexual activity can start labour, when the baby is ready to be born. There may be some basis to this. Semen has natural prostaglandins (hormones) in it, and may stimulate the cervix to 'ripen' a little more. Sexual stimulation in the woman releases hormones — oxytocins — which are released in labour, too. There's no evidence that any sexual activity starts labour too soon. If labour was about to begin anyway, then this helps it a little.

The first stage

WHAT'S HAPPENING?

Labour is usually divided into three stages. The first stage is usually the longest, but anything between an hour and 20 hours or longer is normal.

At the start of the first stage, you may be getting one contraction of 40 or 50 seconds every 10 minutes. At the end, each contraction will usually last longer than a minute, and there will be a gap of no more than a minute between each one. This pattern may vary, though.

Contractions help to open the cervix. When open, contractions help the uterus to push the baby out. By the end of the first stage, the cervix is fully open, and is completely taken up by the uterus.

At 10 centimetres dilated your cervix is fully dilated, and you are ready for the birth.

At the beginning, labour often progresses quite slowly. When you are five to six centimetres dilated, contractions are longer and stronger and labour progresses more quickly. This is called 'established' labour.

Labour probably begins as a result of hormonal impulses, triggered by the baby — we don't know for sure. When the baby's adrenal gland is mature, the baby secretes cortisone. This alters the levels of oestrogen and progesterone in the mother, and as a result she starts to produce hormone-like chemicals called prostaglandins. These stimulate the uterus to start contracting.

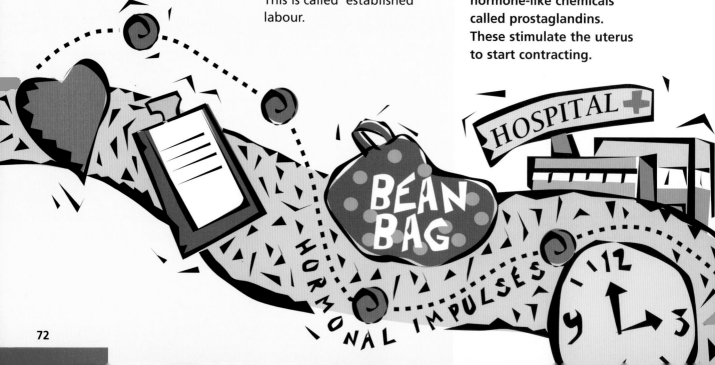

COPING WITH LABOUR

Labour is like a journey up a high, arduous mountain or some other challenge you've faced. Sometimes, you may be able to view the peak. At other times it is hidden, and you may forget the aim of the whole exercise. But each step takes you closer to the peak.

Contractions are steps on that journey. Think of each contraction as a means to an end ... bringing you closer to the birth of your baby. Contractions are usually painful, but between contractions you probably won't feel much pain at all.

starting labour

As you feel a contraction coming ...

- relax. Think especially about your shoulders, your face, your hands. Make sure they are 'unclenched'

- start to concentrate on your breathing, keeping it slow and relaxed. Focus on breathing out

- as the contraction gets stronger, think more carefully about the way you breathe and try to stay relaxed

- sway and rock your pelvis; make any noises you find helpful

- don't resist the contraction — it increases in intensity, it reaches its height, it starts to fade ...

- ... as it goes, blow it away. It's gone. That contraction will never appear again, and it's one less on your journey.

Q. **Can I eat in labour?**

A. It's up to you. You probably won't be hungry when you're in established labour, but you may be earlier on. You will benefit from high-energy, high-carbohydrate snacks, such as honey and crackers, and fluids. Even if you are not hungry, try to drink something to keep your fluid levels and your energy levels up.

The traditional 'rule' on food in labour was that women should not eat anything, just in case they needed a general anaesthetic. In some units, this rule is now relaxed.

Most women cope best with labour if they are not restricted in their movements. You may find different positions — kneeling, leaning forwards on a beanbag or your partner's lap, on all fours and anything else that helps — work best for you at different times. Listen to your body, experiment with different movements, do what's most helpful for you.

MONITORING YOUR BABY

Measuring the baby's heart rate is a way of assessing your baby's health and strength throughout labour and birth.

Different ways of monitoring

- **A Pinard stethoscope** is a type of ear-trumpet, placed against your abdomen to listen to the baby's heart. It is used from time to time during labour.

- **A 'doppler'** is a smaller, portable machine using ultrasound for monitoring at intervals. A small transmitter-receiver is placed on your abdomen to pick up the heartbeat.

- **Electronic fetal monitoring (EFM)** uses ultrasound waves to transmit your baby's heart rate to a machine via a 'transducer' held against your abdomen. Alternatively, a small electrode can be clipped on to your baby's scalp (or the bottom, in a breech baby) and this picks up and transmits the heartbeat. The heart rate usually appears in digital form on the screen, and a record is traced on graph paper and printed out.

- **Telemetry** uses the same sort of transducer or scalp electrode, but sends signals by radio waves to the receiver. You're not actually attached to the monitor by wires, so you are free to move around as long as you stay within its range.

Electronic fetal monitoring

EFM provides continuous monitoring of the baby. In individual cases, this can be important — when the baby is at risk, or if it's known that there could be a problem.

Continuous EFM is not very useful in uncomplicated labour. Interpreting the monitor reading is a highly skilled job. Even very experienced obstetricians differ about what is a 'normal' reading, and what might give cause for concern. In many hospitals, doctors and midwives agree that continuous EFM is not needed for routine,

normal labour, especially not in the first stage. Instead, mothers may be offered monitoring when first admitted to hospital, at intervals afterwards, and during the second stage.

If you and your carers expect everything to be normal, you may prefer to have the other forms of monitoring — intermittent monitoring with a doppler, or a Pinard stethoscope. You'll probably find your baby's heart is listened to every 15 or 20 minutes or so, and after most contractions in second stage.

OTHER CHECKS YOU WILL HAVE

Your condition and the baby's will be assessed when you are admitted to the labour ward, and at intervals throughout the first stage. These are the things which are regularly assessed:

- your blood pressure, your pulse and your temperature

- your urine, which helps the midwife to check your energy levels

- the length, strength and frequency of your contractions

- your cervix, during an internal or vaginal examination. Today, many midwives avoid vaginal examination as a routine. They do this only if they feel the information it gives will be useful.

WHAT IF CONTRACTIONS SLOW DOWN OR STOP?

Sometimes, labour seems to come to a stop. If you and your baby are well, there is no need for concern. Be patient, walk around, change your position, relax with some music ... your contractions will probably start up again in time. You may feel you want to eat something. This is your body's way of telling you that you need more 'fuel' to keep going.

If your labour is very slow, and perhaps because your baby is showing signs of distress, your doctor may advise speeding up your labour. This is called **augmentation** or **acceleration** of labour.

- Your contractions may be stimulated by artificial rupture of the membranes (ARM) if your waters are still unbroken.

- You may be offered a hormone drip, which puts syntocinon directly into your bloodstream. The effect can be quite powerful — the contractions become much stronger than before and more frequent. You may not want this — most mothers cope better with a gradual build-up.

Unless it's essential that things speed up, you may prefer not to have any interventions.

An 'extra' stage of labour, sometimes known as 'transition' comes between first and second stage. Many women clearly experience it as different from other parts of their labour. You may feel the beginning of an urge to push. Alternatively, labour seems to stop.

Transition is a psychological state as well as a physical one. You might feel impatient, and tired, even angry, frustrated or irritable with your carers. This is a perfectly natural reaction and it also means that the birth of your baby is not far off.

YOUR POSITION

All-fours: you can rest by leaning forward between contractions.

Supported standing or squatting allows your pelvis to open wide, and your baby to be born with the help of the force of gravity. You will need support for your upper body to keep your balance or your partner can support you by holding you from behind, under your arms, though it will need strength to take all your weight. Your knees must never be higher than your hips — this would put too much strain on your joints.

On your side: you lie on your side (the 'lateral' position), with your upper leg raised. This is quite helpful if you are extremely tired.

There's no right or wrong position. However, lying on your back is usually uncomfortable and closes your pelvis. When women are encouraged to do what feels best, they hardly ever adopt this position.

Sitting: astride a chair and leaning forward, resting on a cushion or pillow.

first stage

Sitting up in bed is an alternative to lying down but still puts some pressure on the pelvis. If you choose this position use plenty of pillows to support your back and shoulders. Your partner can easily hold you, supporting you behind the shoulders while sitting next to the bed.

The second stage

YOUR BABY'S ALMOST HERE

Second stage begins when the cervix is fully dilated, and ends with the birth of the baby.

You will probably feel a powerful need to push down. It's called 'bearing down'. You may feel when the time is right to push, or your midwife can guide you. You may want to push about three times in each contraction. If you want to hold your breath to bear down, don't hold it too long.

Some women don't feel the urge to bear down, and in some labours it isn't necessary — the baby is born without any effort. If you have an epidural, you may not feel the urge to push, or not as strongly. The midwife will

tell you when you should bear down.

As the head stretches the birth canal and the perineum (the skin between the birth canal and the anus), you may feel a powerful, burning sensation. It only lasts a short time. When the head can be seen completely at the vulva, it is said to be 'crowning'.

You can hold a mirror up if you want to, so you can see this moment.

You may feel your perineum stretching at this point. If there is a risk of tearing the perineum, your carers may ask you not to push now. You may be asked to pant, or to push more gently — to 'breathe the baby out' with lighter, gentler breaths.

With the next contraction or two, your baby's head comes out, and then your baby's body is born.

THE MOMENT OF BIRTH

During second stage, your baby's head turns, usually from facing to one side to facing towards your back.

As your baby's head comes out, the midwife may feel for the umbilical cord, to make sure it is not round the neck. You may be asked to relax or to pant at this point.

The shoulders turn so the body is sideways on, and the head, now fully born, faces towards your leg. Your baby then comes out easily and quickly.

HOW YOUR BABY LOOKS AT BIRTH

Your baby may have vernix on the skin — a creamy substance which helped to moisturise the skin in the uterus. There may be a few streaks of blood on the body (your blood, from your episiotomy or tear if you had one). The baby's head may look slightly misshapen, but this won't last long. It's called moulding — the soft bones of the skull have shaped themselves so that the baby's head can pass through the birth canal.

questions Q&A answered

Q. I know most fathers just take it for granted that they are going to be there during labour and birth. But I can't bear the idea. I know I'll be okay about the baby, and I'm looking forward to being a father. I just don't want to see it happen.

A. It's worth working out why you don't want to be there. Are you worried about being squeamish or even fainting? Or do you feel you won't want to look at the moment of birth, seeing the baby emerge? Or do you worry about what you're supposed to do, and whether you'll do it wrong? All these anxieties are common, and normal.

Talk over your feelings with your partner. If you decide to be there, you can always look away, and concentrate on your partner's face if watching the 'birth end' gets too much. You can leave the room if you need to.

During labour, you may not actually 'do' very much at times. That doesn't matter. Being there is more important. If you end up deciding you won't be there, your partner may need someone who can support her at the birth, and someone who can go to classes with her.

How long does second stage last?

With a first baby, the second stage can last between 10 minutes and a couple of hours or longer. Second or other babies may come after just a few pushes and one or two contractions.

birth

ASSISTING BIRTH

In some situations, forceps or ventouse (vacuum) extraction are used to assist the baby's birth. It can happen when:

● the baby is short of oxygen — called fetal distress. It's diagnosed when the baby's heart rate slows in response to contractions, and doesn't speed up again as it should. A further sign is if the baby's bowels open and pass meconium (the contents of the baby's bowels). This will stain the amniotic fluid a green or brown colour. A small blood sample taken from the baby's scalp can be looked at and measured for oxygen

● the baby's exit is blocked or hampered — the position may be difficult, such as face-up (occipito-posterior), or the mother's pelvis may not be able to open wide enough, sometimes due to her position

● contractions have weakened

● the baby is pre-term, which means the head needs more protection

● the baby is breech, which may mean the head needs protection

● the mother is too tired to push

● the mother has a condition such as a heart disorder, and should not push for too long.

If you need help with forceps or ventouse

You will probably be asked to lie down on your back, and your legs will be raised, with the ankles supported in stirrups.

You will be given an anaesthetic, most likely an epidural or a spinal, or a local anaesthetic called a pudendal block, though a general anaesthetic is very occasionally used. Your bladder may be emptied with a catheter. You will probably need an episiotomy to allow room for the instrument to be inserted.

Forceps are made of two separate halves which lock on to one another. They have handles at one end, and two scoop-like blades at the other. The forceps are inserted into the vagina, one blade at a time. Each blade fits snugly over the sides of the baby's head, cupping it. The handles then lock, forming a protective cage round the head. The forceps turn the baby (if necessary).

Then, as you feel each contraction coming you push, just as you were doing, and the doctor coordinates the pulling.

Q. Will I need stitches after the birth?

A. Sometimes the perineum tears while stretching over the baby's head. Or the midwife may ask if she can cut the perineum because you are about to tear badly, or the baby needs to be born quickly. This cut is known as an 'episiotomy'. There is some difference of opinion among midwives as to how often one should be done, although most would agree that it should only be used as an emergency procedure.

A small tear usually heals itself. Larger ones, and episiotomies, may need stitching. You will be given a local anaesthetic while this is done. The stitches should dissolve themselves — you don't usually need to have them taken out. Until this happens, it's normal to have a few days of discomfort when you sit down. Tell the midwife if you have more pain than this. Sometimes taking out a stitch or two can help.

Ventouse extraction can turn and deliver the baby. It has a tube with a cup on it at one end. The tube leads to a small vacuum pump. The cup is attached to the baby's head by suction. The mother pushes with each contraction and the doctor pulls.

Your baby may show bruising on each side of the head where the forceps have been. Vacuum extraction can cause swelling (sometimes called a 'chignon') on the head. None of this is permanent, and it will disappear over the next few days.

The third stage

YOUR BABY IS BORN

The third stage of labour is the delivery of the placenta and the membranes after your baby's birth. For most women, the third stage passes uneventfully. You might hardly be aware of it happening. In most hospitals the third stage is **'actively managed'**. This means some actions are routinely taken to speed up this stage of labour.

- First, you may have an injection to cause the uterus to contract. It is given when your baby is being born, usually when the first shoulder is coming out. The injection goes into your thigh or your buttock. The midwife will ask you for your consent before she does it.

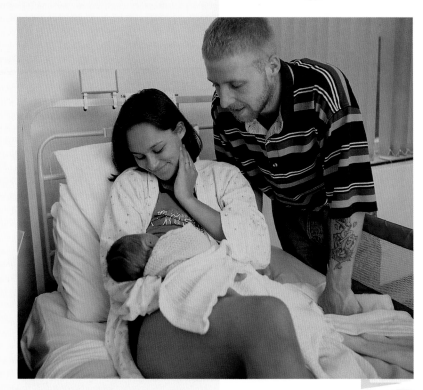

- The second action happens when your baby is born. The umbilical cord is clamped and cut. It's usual to make sure that the baby is breathing well, and is no longer dependent on the placenta for oxygen. **If you have not had an injection** the cord may

be cut now, or left until it stops pulsating or until after the delivery of the placenta.

- As the injection now takes effect, it stimulates the uterus into contracting very strongly, becoming smaller, harder and tighter. This causes the placenta to peel off the inner wall of the uterus. The contraction may make you want to push again, and you may be able to push the placenta out. More usually, the doctor or midwife helps the delivery of the placenta. They put one hand on your abdomen to protect the uterus, while keeping the cord taut with the other hand. This is called 'cord traction'.

● The placenta comes away and the blood vessels which were 'holding on' to the placenta close off as the muscle in your uterus contracts. This prevents bleeding (though it's normal to bleed a little). You may feel the placenta slide down and out between your legs, followed by the membranes.

Occasionally, the placenta does not come away from the uterus. When this happens, the mother needs a small operation to remove it, which is always done under anaesthetic.

Another possible complication of the third stage is bleeding, called 'postpartum haemorrhage' or PPH. A haemorrhage needs to be treated immediately.

A speeded up or 'actively-managed' third stage lasts between 10 and 20 minutes. An unaided, or natural (also called 'physiological'), third stage can take longer. It happens without an injection or cord traction.

The action of feeding your baby at the breast, or simply having the baby there, stimulates the release of the hormone oxytocin. This helps your uterus to contract, to push out the placenta and membranes. It can help to be upright, to make use of gravity.

The cord is cut when it stops pulsating, and often after the placenta is delivered.

You may want to discuss the third stage and whether it's managed or not, when making your birth plan. If you have problems during the first and/or second stage, a natural third stage may not be a safe option.

YOUR BABY'S FIRST MOMENTS

Your baby's Apgar score: shortly after the birth, the midwife will assess your baby's well-being with the Apgar score. It's done by observation, most commonly at one minute and five minutes after the birth. Some units do a two minute assessment only.

The midwife looks at the baby's condition, and gives a 'score' of 0, 1 or 2 for these aspects of the baby's appearance and health.

Table of scores
Apgar score

	0	1	2
breathing	Absent	Weak/Irregular	Regular
colour	Blue or pale	Blue extremities	Pink
muscle tone	Absent	Some flexion	Active movement
response to stimulation	Absent	Weak movement	Cries
heart rate	Absent	Less than 100 bpm	More than 100 bpm

2 = normal

A top score is 10, and most healthy babies score at least seven. A score of five or less is poor, and means the baby needs some form of resuscitation.

first moments

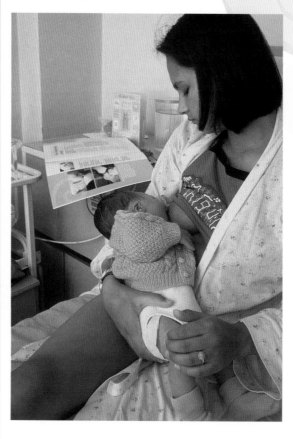

YOUR BABY'S FIRST FEED

If your baby is alert and healthy, you can offer the first breastfeed as soon as she or he is born. A baby who isn't really interested in sucking or feeding — and some just aren't — can enjoy being held close, getting to know their mother's skin, smell and taste.

If your baby is interested, the midwife will usually guide you to position your baby in a way that's comfortable, and which allows the baby to feed well. Feeding shouldn't nip or hurt (see page 99).

Hold your baby and see the way he or she looks at you, gazing at you, as if you really are getting to know each other. You'll probably find you talk to your baby, and take great pleasure in studying him or her all over, watching every movement and expression.

Caesarean birth

WHY IT'S DONE AND WHAT HAPPENS

A Caesarean birth means your baby is born by an operation. The surgeon makes an opening in your abdomen and then the uterus. In your notes, you may see it as LSCS, or LUSCS, which is the abbreviation for Lower Segment Caesarean Section, or Lower Uterine Segment Caesarean Section, or simply as CS (Caesarean Section).

You may know in advance that you will have a Caesarean section. You'll probably have it before you go into labour, so your appointment will be before your expected date of delivery. This advance planning is called an 'elective section'. Some women need a Caesarean section after going into labour and expecting to give birth

vaginally. This is called an emergency Caesarean section, although most cases are not as dramatic and last-minute as that sounds.

What happens to you

The operation is the same whatever type of anaesthetic you have. It's more common today to have an anaesthetic — a spinal or an epidural — which allows you to stay awake, though you should not feel any pain. Your partner or birth companion can usually be with you.

The surgeon first makes a cut at the base of your abdomen and then through the uterus, in a line just above your pubic hair.

You may feel some tugging when the baby is lifted out, sometimes by hand, sometimes with a pair of forceps. The baby's umbilical cord is cut and clamped, and if all is well he or she will be given to you (if you are conscious) to hold. The placenta and membranes are delivered next, and then your uterus and abdomen are stitched. It only takes about 10 minutes to deliver the baby and about 30 minutes to stitch you afterwards.

Caesarean

The reasons why you may decide on a Caesarean section include:

- you have a very low-lying placenta (called placenta praevia) which blocks your baby's way out

- multiple pregnancy — for some twins and almost always for triplets or more

- other complications, such as previous surgery on the vagina

- malpresentation — your baby is in a position which makes vaginal birth difficult or impossible.

Reasons for an emergency Caesarean section include:

- eclampsia or severe pre-eclampsia in the mother (see pages 55–56) means the pregnancy should end as soon as possible

- sudden onset of severe illness, such as kidney disease, or very high blood pressure

- the baby is in a poor or impossible position for birth ('malpresentation') or is too big to come out through the pelvis safely ('disproportion'). This may not have been apparent until labour had begun

- the baby is suffering from fetal distress (lack of oxygen) and labour hasn't progressed enough for a forceps or a ventouse delivery

- to avoid a difficult forceps delivery

- your baby's head is too big for your pelvis, or your pelvis shape or size won't allow the baby to be born without major difficulty

- lack of progress in labour, when the contractions are weak and the cervix doesn't dilate

- the mother is exhausted after a long, difficult labour.

Anaesthesia and Caesarean section

If you have a Caesarean section you will need total pain relief. Some women have a general anaesthetic, which means you are unconscious during the operation. Other women have an epidural or spinal anaesthetic. This completely numbs you from the site of the injection downwards, but allows you to remain fully awake and aware of everything but the pain.

You take time to recover from the effects of a general anaesthetic and there are more risks to the mother's health. So where there is a choice mothers usually opt for epidural or spinal anaesthesia. In some units, doctors administer a combined spinal and epidural which allows a top-up of anaesthetic when necessary.

AFTER YOUR SECTION

In the first days after your Caesarean section, you will feel very tired — probably more tired than after a vaginal birth — and you may have some pain, especially round your wound. You may suffer from intestinal wind, which is common after any abdominal operation. Laughing or coughing may hurt, too. The midwife will show you how to support your wound when you need to cough or laugh to avoid any pressure on your tummy. Wear large pants that come up to your waist, rather than briefs whose elastic may rub against your scar. You'll be offered pain-relief which is safe to take while breastfeeding.

You may be fitted with a small drain which collects any blood that might otherwise pool under the wound. This is usually removed in a day or so. At first, an intravenous drip in your arm will replace lost fluids. You won't be able to get up to pass urine, and you will either have a catheter, or be helped to use a bedpan.

The stitches in your skin may simply dissolve or be removed later. Individual clips will also be removed.

q u e s t i o n s   Q&A   a n s w e r e d

Q. **Will I need a Caesarean section if I have another baby?**

A. **Probably not, unless the reason for your Caesarean section occurs again, or if you produce a big baby and you have a small pelvis ('disproportion'). However, the diagnosis of disproportion is not always hard and fast, and you may want to ask for a second opinion.**

If you go into labour, there is a slight risk that contractions may cause the scar on your uterus to start to tear. Although this is rare and can happen without warning, with proper care, this can be spotted before it becomes a problem.

Your feelings

Sometimes, women feel disappointed if they've had a Caesarean birth. To have the baby delivered 'for' you, can make you feel you have missed out on something essential. Then, if the baby is fine, you may feel guilty at being disappointed. Talk about these feelings with your partner, with your midwife, and with other mothers who have had Caesarean births. Understanding why you needed a Caesarean section can help you put the experience in perspective. Support organisations may help (see **Further help** at the back of this book).

Breastfeeding after a Caesarean section

Breastfeeding your baby sometimes needs patience. You need help to hold your baby comfortably, and to be comfortable yourself, without pressure on your tummy. Raising your baby on a pillow across your lap is one way, or try feeding lying on your side.

If you have had a Caesarean section your breast milk may take four or five days to 'come in'. Don't worry about this. It won't affect breastfeeding in the long term at all.

The first days

CHANGES IN YOUR BABY

At first, your baby may look a little odd — even squashed and wrinkly, and possibly bluish on the hands and feet. Over the next few days, you'll notice the skin seems to smooth out a little, the head becomes rounder, and the whitish skin coating of vernix disappears.

Some babies sleep quite a lot in the first two or three days; others are quite alert. Later, though, most babies become more wakeful, and need more feeds and more care generally.

CHECKS YOUR BABY MAY HAVE

In the first days after the birth, checks are offered to make sure your baby is healthy. The doctor or midwife will discuss them with you beforehand.

- **Heart.** If you are told your baby has an additional sound of the heart called a 'murmur', you may feel worried, but in fact the condition is very common. One estimate is that 50 per cent of babies have a heart murmur in the first week. Within a few weeks, most murmurs are not heard any more.

- **Congenital dislocation of the hip.** The doctor examines each hip joint to check that the head of the thigh bone (femur) moves as it should do within the socket for the femur at the hip, and that it doesn't slip out.

- **PKU — phenylketonuria.** A very rare (1 in 10,000) metabolic disorder. The 'Guthrie' test is carried out in the first week or so of life, usually after the fifth day, to check for this and some other rare conditions. Your baby's heel is pricked, and several drops of blood are placed on a special card. This is then sent to the laboratory so the samples of blood can be tested. Ask the midwife what the tests will show.

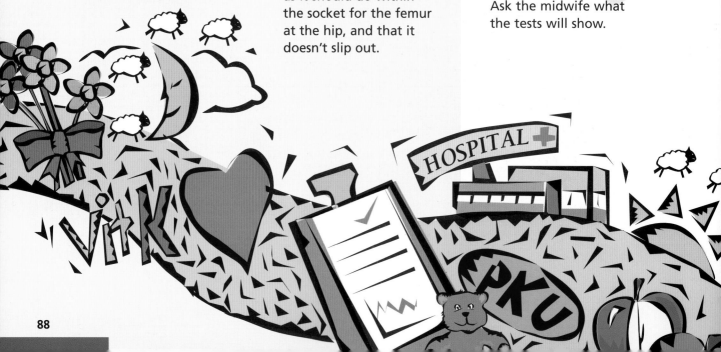

- **Jaundice**. Checked usually just by observing the skin, which is yellowish if the baby has it. Many new babies have mild jaundice, caused by a substance called bilirubin still present in the blood. If the yellow colour of the skin doesn't go away, a blood check is done to see whether the jaundice is severe or not.

In most units, Vitamin K for your baby is offered routinely, shortly after birth, either orally (by mouth) or by injection. This is to prevent a rare condition called haemorrhagic disease of the newborn, when the blood fails to clot. You should be given as much information as you wish about this, and be asked for permission before Vitamin K is given. Research is still being done on the effectiveness and safety of Vitamin K. Some experts have argued that not enough is known about the levels of Vitamin K in the normal, healthy newborn.

Reflexes checked for include:

- **the Moro or 'startle' reflex**. Your baby is supported on the tester's hand and forearm, and when the tester's hand is taken away from the head, the baby flings out his or her arms and legs, and then slowly settles back into position

- **the stepping response** comes if you hold your baby in a 'standing' position — both hands round the chest and facing away from you. Place one of the baby's feet on a hard surface (like a table). The leg of that foot extends, and the other leg moves forward, as if your baby was taking a step

- **the trunk incurvation reflex**. You will see this reflex if you stroke your baby's back firmly, following down the line of the spine, and the baby's back will curve.

FROM THE MOMENT OF BIRTH, YOUR BABY CAN:

- **see**, though focusing on objects more than about 25 cm (10 inches) away is difficult. The baby's eyes will follow your face, if you hold him or her up while you look at each other, and then turn your head

- **hear,** and be startled by loud noises. The baby seems to respond best to soft, light voices — the sort of tone most of us use instinctively when we are talking to a new baby

- **grasp,** seen if you touch the baby's palm. The toes will be flexed, too, if you stroke the soles of the baby's feet.

REGISTERING THE BIRTH

In Scotland, you must register your baby's birth within three weeks. The hospital or midwife notifies the local Child Health Unit within 36 hours, which in turn notifies the Registrar of births and your health visitor. You will receive a reminder if you don't register the birth within this time. If you are married to your baby's father, either of you can register your baby. If you are not married, and you want the baby's father to have his name on the certificate, then you need to go together to register the birth.

TAKING YOUR BABY HOME

Home from special care

You may find your relief at coming home is mixed with nervousness. Some of this is the same anxiety that all new parents feel at this big step, but you have the added concern that your baby may still be quite small.

You will stay in touch with your baby's hospital paediatrician for a time, either directly, or through a neonatal nurse working in the community. You will already have met your nurse when your baby was in special care.

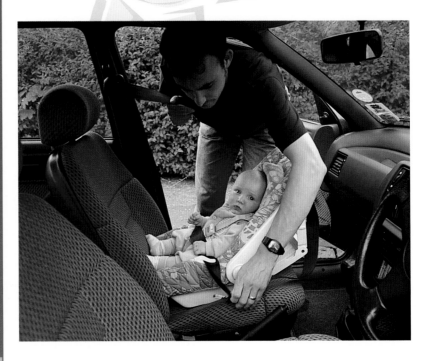

Remember car safety

You should use an appropriate child restraint on every journey including the one home from the hospital. It is dangerous to sit with your baby on your lap or in your arms. All persons in a vehicle must wear a restraining harness (seat belt) at all times when the vehicle is moving.

A special baby seat can be used in either the front or back seat. It must be held in place by an adult seat belt. You can't use it with a seat belt that just goes over your lap.

If you have an airbag fitted on the passenger side your baby **must** travel in the back seat.

Learn how to fit and remove the seat before you use it with the baby. Some hospitals hire baby car seats. Some taxi services also supply a baby seat — ask for this special service if you ever use a taxi for you and your baby, and you don't have your own seat. (See also page 131.)

> **NEVER put your seat belt around yourself AND your baby**

Your life after the birth

CHANGES YOU CAN EXPECT

Immediately after the birth, your tummy will look saggy and soft. Most women regain their pre-pregnancy weight and shape simply by eating normally — though you may never look **exactly** the same. Exercise may speed things up, and it's important to do the pelvic floor exercises to restore tone to this area (see page 92). If you have had a Caesarean section or split abdominal muscle some exercises may not be suitable for you — ask your midwife or an obstetric physiotherapist.

The uterus still contracts in the days after birth, as it goes back to its pre-pregnancy size. You may sometimes feel these contractions (known as 'afterpains'). If you find them too painful (not everyone does) ask the midwife or GP which painkillers are safe to take.

Your breasts may increase in size and feel more tender

when your milk comes in (see page 100). This is a result of the increase in milk, blood and lymph in the breast tissue.

Vaginal discharge (lochia) after childbirth is a mix of blood and other material squeezed out of the uterus. At first it's bright red, then pinkish brown, through to cream. It's quite heavy at first and you will need several changes of sanitary pads a day (tampons are not recommended, because of the risk of infection). During the first 24 hours some women find disposable nappies more effective than sanitary pads.

After the first week it slows down a lot, but you may find it lasts three or four weeks before finally disappearing. Get medical advice if you start to lose fresh red blood when your bleeding has previously been brown, or if the discharge is smelly, or if you have abdominal pain, or a temperature. However, some fresh red blood loss is normal after a breastfeed.

Constipation for a couple of days is very common after childbirth. Help yourself by drinking plenty of fluids and eating high-fibre foods, including fresh fruit and vegetables.

The six-week postnatal check

Around six weeks after the birth, you'll be invited to see either your GP, the community midwife, or a doctor at the unit where your baby was born.

This is a routine assessment, done to make sure you are returning to normal physically, and that if you're not, any problems can be dealt with. It's also an opportunity to ask you how you feel, and to answer any questions you may have. You can also talk about contraception at this check-up if you want.

The doctor may suggest doing an internal examination, and palpate your abdomen, to make sure the uterus has returned to its pre-pregnancy size. If you don't feel ready for this, say so.

afterwards

'I felt this pressure to get back to normal — and I wanted some time and space to myself. I found the baby just totally overwhelming — I couldn't stop being worried about her, and scared I was doing everything wrong.'

'Baby blues'

'Postnatal blues' or 'baby blues' is a very common feeling of tearfulness, around two or three days after the birth. It's rather like coming down to earth after the 'high' of giving birth. It could also be hormonal, as this is about the time the mature milk 'comes in'. You may find yourself weeping, and feeling 'at sea' among your new emotions. It usually passes after a day or so, but you will need extra support while it lasts (see also pages 96–98 on postnatal depression).

Pelvic floor exercises

Pelvic floor exercises can help you regain the tone in these important muscles. They help prevent the stress incontinence (see page 52) that can occur after childbirth (causing you to leak a few drops of urine when you cough, laugh or run). You may not feel you have any control over your pelvic floor muscles immediately after birth and for the next couple of days.

Remember, the more often you do them, the better! You'll be taught how to do them in pregnancy or after birth by a midwife or a physiotherapist. Start in the first days after the birth, and aim for four or five sets of 10 or 12 exercises each day. You can do them at any time — in fact it's a good idea to get into the habit of doing them every day of your life, and to make them a part

of your routine. It may be helpful to form the habit by remembering to do them **after** you pass urine each time.

Do them gently at first.

1. **Imagine you are trying to stop yourself passing urine. Tighten your front passage to prevent leaking.**

2. **Relax slowly, as you breathe out.**

3. **Repeat.**

If your pelvic floor muscles are weak you may find this quite difficult at first. With frequent practice, though, you will soon improve. If you don't, see your GP. To check if your muscles are effective, try stopping the passage of urine in mid-stream. Do not do this too often, just once every few weeks will be enough.

YOUR RELATIONSHIPS, YOUR LIFE

Many things change after the birth. You may feel you have begun a whole new phase in your life, yet all the world's attention seems to be on your baby's needs, and not your own. Your greatest needs will include time, and adult support and conversation. You may feel your life has been taken over by the baby. If anyone offers to help, think of something they can do — or they may never ask again! Most people are delighted to think they can do you a small favour, and enjoy sharing in the upheaval a new baby brings.

Your partner

Trust your partner to care for the baby, and share your pleasures and anxieties. Spend time alone, if you can, as a couple — though this may not be easy to achieve for a while!

Your family and friends

Offers of help and support may be welcome, but don't feel you have to entertain them when they visit. If you find it tiring to see people, don't be afraid to ask visitors to come another time, or else arrange to visit them.

'People relate to you differently when you've had a baby. I feel my friends are more interested in the baby than me! I suppose they could be thinking "Maybe I'll be next".'

'My main memory of those first few weeks was being tired — every night was broken, usually more than once. Sometimes, the crying went on for hours. That wears you down. It was great when we could see he was growing out of it. You feel you must be doing something wrong, even when people tell you you're not.'
(Partner)

'It took a while to get close to the baby. It was great after she was born, and I know I loved her, but I don't think I had what you might call a "relationship" with her for ages. I only really started to enjoy her when she was a few months old, and showed me that she enjoyed being with me ... she gets excited when she hears me come in, and holds her arms out to me to be picked up. I love that!'
(Partner)

Making new friends

In most areas there are groups of other parents whose support and friendship can be a great help. If you're shy, it can be hard to break into these networks, so you may need to be quite brave and patient. Some organisations have coffee groups, or drop-in centres, or toddler clubs. Ring up to check on time and place of a meeting. Say who you are, ask who they are, and then ask for them by name when you get there. At least that way, you'll feel you know (or sort of know) someone. Don't be put off if you've picked a group that seems like a clique. That does happen, unfortunately. Either try again, or try another group.

Your health visitor will know of other people you can meet, and put you in touch, and will be a good source of information about different clubs. A health visitor can help you start your own group, if there's nothing to suit you.

q u e s t i o n s   a n s w e r e d

Q. **Does breastfeeding act as a contraceptive?**

A. **Breastfeeding may affect ovulation, which means you are less likely to produce an egg. You are less likely to conceive, and your periods are suppressed.**

One method of contraception uses the fact that breastfeeding (lactation) means you may not menstruate ('amenorrhoea' means no menstruation). It is called the 'lactational amenorrhoea' method of family planning.

If you want to use this method as a contraceptive, speak to a counsellor or a doctor. For this to work you need to breastfeed exclusively and often, without giving any bottles, including through the night. **Even so, there is no guarantee you won't conceive using this method. If you want to be sure of avoiding a pregnancy, you need to use another form of contraception.** Ovulation happens before menstruation, so your fertility can return without you realising.

Some women don't menstruate when they are breastfeeding — even when the baby is older, and well-established on solid food, perhaps feeding only once or twice a day. Other women find their periods return when their baby starts to space feeds, or begins taking anything other than breast milk. Some start as early as a few weeks after the birth.

Sex after childbirth

You may be asked about contraception choices very soon after the birth — maybe when sex is absolutely the very last thing on your mind! Health professionals raise the topic so that you have time to think about this before the decision becomes more pressing. You can get advice at any time, though, from your doctor, health visitor or family planning clinic.

If you are breastfeeding, you'll be advised to avoid the combined pill — the sort that contains oestrogen and progesterone. This is because oestrogen may reduce the amount of milk you produce. The progesterone-only pill (sometimes known as the mini-pill) is more suitable (see also 'Family Planning' in the **Further help** section).

If you resume intercourse, you should start using your chosen method of contraception within four weeks of the birth to ensure protection. If you use a diaphragm or a cap, you should get it checked, to make sure it still fits (the cervix can change size and shape slightly after birth).

For many women a condom may be the simplest choice for the early weeks after childbirth.

If sex hurts, see your doctor about this. If you feel too 'dry' for sex, use a lubricant like KY Jelly. This is safe to use with a condom or diaphragm, as oil-based lubricants can damage them.

How soon should you, or can you, start making love after the birth — and what if you don't want to?

Physically, there's no reason why you shouldn't make love as soon as the lochia (discharge) has ceased and any cut or tear in the perineum has healed (before then, there may be a risk of infection). In practice, you may want to wait longer — both men and women vary a lot in how soon they want to resume their sex life. Remember, either or both of you may just feel too tired for sex — this is quite normal.

Be patient with yourselves. If you are breastfeeding, your breasts and nipples may be tender at first. If you've been stitched, you may feel bruised and battered for a while. Emotionally, a long, tiring or difficult labour can make you feel less ready to share your body.

Keep in physical and emotional touch with each other. Arrange special times for love-making — you can't be as spontaneous as you were, when you have a baby who may need your attention at any time.

Even if you can't, or don't want to, make love properly or fully, you can show your love for each other in many different, sensual ways — share a special dinner (or take-away) and leave the washing-up until the next day; give each other a sensuous massage.

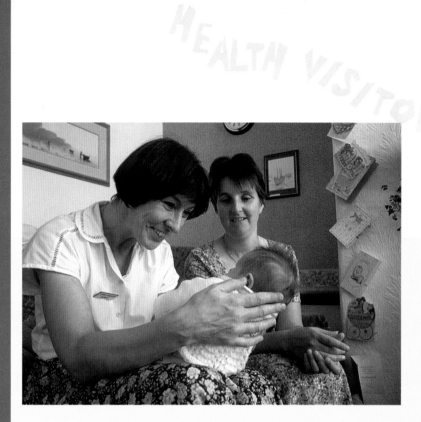

SUPPORT FOR YOU AND YOUR BABY

The midwife is responsible for your care for the first 10 days after the birth, and can extend this for longer, if needed. In practice, hospital midwives transfer your care to the community, and one or more community midwives will visit you at home after you have left hospital. The schedule of visits can be discussed between you and the midwife.

Very often the midwife transfers your care to the health visitor after the tenth day. Your health visitor will visit you and your baby soon after. One of the health visitor's responsibilities is to care for families with children under five (see also pages 37 and 122).

You should have a phone number to call a midwife and a health visitor if you need help outside normal working hours. Your health visitor will give you a number to call. She will also tell you about the baby clinic, and when you can bring your baby for immunisations. She may give you a child health record, a booklet for keeping information about your baby's growth, health, immunisations, and so on.

If you had a difficult birth, you may find yourself thinking about it a lot, perhaps wondering why it happened. It can help to talk about it with someone who understands pregnancy and childbirth, and who can explain some of the technical side to you. You, your GP or your midwife or health visitor can get hold of your notes if you don't have them, and you can go through the written account together.

Postnatal depression

WHY DOES IT HAPPEN AND WHAT CAN BE DONE?

Postnatal depression (PND) is a very complex issue and the root causes are not known. It would be very difficult to identify any specific causes especially biological ones.

In a busy, modern and competitive world, the cause of PND may have something to do with the way our society treats new mothers, who may not get the support they need. They may feel friendless, and worthless, as social contacts are hard to keep up and even harder to make. The most important treatment for PND may be friendship and social support. Health visitors have been active in offering one-to-one support for depressed mothers, and in setting up groups. At the groups, new mothers with PND (as well as those who are lonely, or bored, or isolated) can get to know each other in an understanding environment, and talk about their situation.

Some studies show that the causes of PND could be hormonal, and some doctors treat mothers with progesterone therapy, or oestrogen therapy. Your doctor may prescribe conventional anti-depressants.

Psychotherapy has also been shown to help. This involves talking to a therapist about the experience of being a mother and what went on in your own childhood and afterwards, too. Sometimes, being a mother touches parts of ourselves we had forgotten about, or hidden away. It's thought that dealing with emotions can help with PND.

HEALTH VISITOR

You may have PND if you have some of the following symptoms:

- time passes you by sometimes — you can look at the clock and wonder where the last two hours went

- you wake up each morning feeling exhausted, as if you haven't had any sleep

- you find you laugh and smile less

- you find it hard to concentrate, or organise simple tasks

- it's hard for you to see 'the funny side' of things

- you sometimes feel numb, as if feelings and experiences don't reach you

- simple tasks may require enormous effort

- you find yourself crying, or feeling tearful, for small things, or for no reason at all

- you feel you can only be yourself with your partner, and sometimes not even then.

Around 1 in 10 new mothers experience PND. Many more — perhaps half — go through spells of feeling loneliness, isolation and exhaustion, or very low and lacking in confidence.

Although PND is better recognised now than it used to be, mothers still sometimes try to hide how bad they feel, and they may blame themselves for feeling that way.

A mother with PND may care for her baby's physical needs perfectly well, and there may be nothing to show of the turmoil and sadness she feels.

Remember that help is available. PND is curable. It is just not worth suffering in silence. If you think you may need help, speak to your health visitor, midwife or doctor.

'I didn't even know I had postnatal depression ... hard to believe now. I had heard of PND, of course, and my cousin had suffered from it, too. But when it came to my own feelings, I knew I just didn't feel right, without really putting a label on myself. I just felt I wasn't a very good mother, that Joseph was a difficult, wakeful baby, and too much for me to cope with. I know I had to drag myself through the day, and that a lot of energy went on trying to act "normal".

'In the end, it was my health visitor who encouraged me to go for help. She recognised that things weren't as they should be, and we talked about what I felt and so on. My doctor helped me, though it took a few months before I felt I was better.'

e m o t i o n s

PUERPERAL PSYCHOSIS

Occasionally, a mother can suffer a severe form of mental illness called puerperal psychosis. It happens to between 1 and 2 in every 1000 new mothers. It's different from PND, and needs different treatment.

Mothers with this illness can lose touch with reality at times. Typically, they have strange ideas, and/or hallucinations. They may be very energetic or else extremely down. It's soon obvious to anyone close to them that they are ill. (This is different from postnatal depression, where it's possible to hide the symptoms for a long time.)

Psychiatric treatment is needed, and the mother will be admitted to hospital, perhaps with her baby if there are the facilities for the baby to be cared for as well.

PARTNERS AND POSTNATAL DEPRESSION

Partners are especially important for women going through postnatal depression. The partner may be the only person a depressed woman can be herself with — and so gets the full impact of her distress. Partners may be angry and need help themselves. Their love and encouragement are essential for recovery, and their insistence on getting help may be the first step on that path. It may help a woman if she has her partner with her when she goes to seek treatment. A partner may be better at remembering what was said during the consultation, to remind her later.

Recent research has suggested that men, too, can suffer depression after they become fathers.

Feeding your baby

WHAT YOU NEED TO KNOW

Breastfeeding

Breast milk is the best food and drink for your baby. It is always high in quality, perfectly adapting itself to your baby's needs for the first four to six months of life. Breastfeeding is natural, but is something both mother and baby may have to learn to do. You need to feel confident, and it helps when the people around you support your choice.

A good start

You can begin breastfeeding as soon as you can after the birth. If your baby is healthy, this can be straight away. Not all babies are interested in feeding at this point, but holding your baby close to get used to your skin, your taste and your smell, is a loving welcome to the world.

When you and your baby are learning, remember these points:

- hold your baby chest to chest — so that the head is opposite your breast and the baby can take your breast without turning. When his or her mouth is as wide open as a yawn, bring the baby gently on to your breast to get a good mouthful. Some of the underneath part of the areola — the dark skin surrounding your nipple —

should go into the mouth, too. This is called getting 'latched' on, or fixed, or attached

- you can help your baby to get well latched on by not slotting your nipple in — as if you were posting a letter. Avoid pushing his or her head on, and don't try to shape your nipple with your fingers. Any of these actions could make your baby take the end of the nipple only. This can lead to sore and cracked nipples, and ineffective feeding. If you have inverted nipples, you may need help to get your baby well latched on.

How it works

As the baby sucks and takes milk from the breasts, hormonal responses 'tell' your body to make more milk. The more you feed, the more milk you make — that's why mothers of twins make twice as much milk. Effective breastfeeding also stimulates the 'let-down' reflex which pushes milk stored deep inside the breast down into the ducts and out through the small outlets on the nipples.

You and your baby are a partnership. Letting your baby establish the timing, length and frequency of feeds means that the right amount of milk is produced. When you are more used to breastfeeding, you can encourage your baby into a routine. But in the early days and weeks, frequent feeds — between 6 and 12 feeds in 24 hours, at irregular intervals — are normal.

Changes in the early days

Your milk adapts to your baby's needs. The milk you produce in pregnancy and for the first few days after the birth is called colostrum. It is a highly-concentrated, straw-coloured fluid, rich in nutrients and antibodies which protect your baby. Your milk 'comes in' between days two and five.

The first milk your baby gets at the start of the feed is called 'foremilk'. As the let-down reflex works, your breasts release fattier, calorie-rich 'hindmilk'. Your baby needs both foremilk and hindmilk to grow and to stay healthy. That's why it's best to leave it up to your baby to decide when she or he has had enough — don't take the baby off the breast after any particular time.

One 'side' or two?

Your baby may take one or both breasts at every feed — it doesn't matter. Let the baby stay on one breast as long as he or she likes, then offer the other. The baby may or may not take it. At the next feed, offer the second, or 'unused', breast first.

Q. Do I need to drink or eat anything special when I am breastfeeding?

A. No. Eat a balanced diet and drink according to thirst. You may be thirstier than usual, especially at first, but don't force yourself to drink more than you want to. Some women find they are a little hungrier, too. Don't avoid any foods unless you are certain they have caused a reaction in your baby. There's no evidence that any particular type of food will have more effect than any other. If you feel your baby reacts to something in your diet, speak to your midwife or health visitor or breastfeeding counsellor.

Some medication is best avoided by breastfeeding mothers. If your doctor prescribes something, say you are breastfeeding. Before taking any over-the-counter remedies, tell the pharmacist you are breastfeeding and check the packaging.

Alcohol in small amounts is not thought to be harmful but your baby's liver will take much longer than yours to break it down.

PEANUTS and foods containing peanut products should continue to be avoided if you or close relatives suffer from eczema, hayfever and asthma.

Breastfeeding protects your baby by building up immunity against a wide range of infections and conditions. Research has shown that breastfed babies have a reduced risk of:

- gastro-enteritis — vomiting and diarrhoea
- ear infections
- wheeze when breathing/asthma
- eczema, where this runs in the family
- developing diabetes in childhood
- urinary infections
- chest infections.

Breast milk has a special value for pre-term babies who are vulnerable to some potentially very dangerous conditions (such as neonatal necrotizing enterocolitis). Breast milk also ensures better brain development in pre-term babies.

Mothers who breastfeed have a reduced risk of:

- ovarian cancer
- pre-menopausal breast cancer
- hip fracture in later life, caused by the bone disease osteoporosis.

When breastfeeding goes well, it's very enjoyable, and both mother and baby find it highly rewarding.

Breastfeeding difficulties

Breastfeeding problems are common, but almost all can be solved. Many are avoidable in the first place, if the baby is attached and positioned at the breast correctly, and if allowed to feed when she or he wants.

Sore nipples: are almost always caused by positioning. Check, and if necessary, correct the way the baby takes the breast, and the baby's position. Sometimes, soreness is caused by thrush on the nipple. Both you and your baby need treatment from the doctor.

Blocked ducts and mastitis: milk is not able to flow through one part of the breast. This means milk collects in the milk secretion and storage tissue (the alveoli). This can cause mastitis — an inflammation of the breast, with or without an infection. Symptoms are a lump, a red patch, pain on feeding and possibly flu-like feverishness in you. Continue feeding, but seek advice from a breastfeeding counsellor, health visitor or midwife. Treatment from the doctor may be necessary — antibiotics prevent/deal with infection which may reduce inflammation.

Not enough milk: increase your supply by feeding more often, checking the way the baby latches on to the breast, and by letting your baby stay on the breast as long as he or she wants to. You may find that making sure to look after yourself, by resting, eating well and reducing stress, can help, too.

Remember, almost every woman is able to make enough milk for her baby. Bottles of water, formula or anything else may reduce your chances of successfully establishing breastfeeding. If bottle feeds fill your baby up, she or he will spend less time at the breast which can reduce the amount of milk you produce.

You can get more information about breastfeeding from some of the organisations listed in the Further help section at the back of this book.

Later breastfeeding

Mothers often say that breastfeeding gets easier after the first weeks. When it's going well you notice the convenience of it. If you have felt embarrassed at breastfeeding in front of others, that disappears as your confidence grows. Your baby latches on quickly, feeds take less time, and your baby may feed less often. You can have time away from your baby when you need to, between feeds.

As time goes on, your milk is produced at the same time as your baby sucks, without a build-up of milk between feeds. If you notice your breasts feel softer and 'emptier' than before, it may mean that your supply is now responsive to the needs of your baby. You can carry on feeding as long as you want to. Once you have been breastfeeding for some months, your milk supply keeps going. One feed a day or less, which may be all a breastfeeding toddler takes, can be enough to maintain your supply.

'I was never very keen on the idea of breastfeeding. I always knew I would find it awkward to feed in front of other people — I guessed I would feel embarrassed. I didn't have much confidence in my ability to produce enough milk, and at least with a bottle you can see how much milk the baby's getting. Then, I thought about the benefits, and promised myself I'd give it a fortnight.

'The first few days were difficult, and I shed a few tears. I was very sore, and my nipples cracked. But it got better, and I had a lot of support from the midwife who helped me to keep going and taught me how to get my baby latched on so my nipples healed. I practised feeding in ways that no-one could actually see what I was doing — I wore T-shirts and tops that pulled up, and found the baby and my clothing hid my breast from view.

'Now he's four months, and I'm still doing it. It's easy now, and I keep thinking of all the work I've saved, not having to sterilise bottles and prepare feeds.'

A word about weight gain

When you let your baby feed as often and as long as he or she wants, you can't see how much breast milk is being taken. The only 'proof' you have of growth is to look at weight gain on the growth chart. If it shows your baby is putting on less weight than expected, this can be worrying for you. But remember, weight charts can be misleading, as they were developed from studying the growth of bottle-fed babies, and also may not apply to all cultures.

weight gain

Weight is only one indicator of a baby's progress. There are others. For example, an alert, healthy baby, who appears content and satisfied after most feeds, and who usually manages to get attached to the breast without a fuss, is giving you signs that breastfeeding is working well.

How do you know your baby is doing okay?

Healthy, well-nourished, breastfed babies:

- manage to get attached to the breast without any fuss at most feeds

- have 5–6 wet nappies every day

- pass soft, yellow stools. The occasional green stool is not usually significant. It's normal for some breastfed babies to go several days between bowel movements ... and it's also normal for some to pass a number of motions a day

- have good muscle tone

- develop as expected (for instance, smiling by about six weeks).

Note: your baby should be weighed without clothing or a nappy every time.

Q. **Is it possible to mix breastfeeding with bottle feeding?**

A. **We know from research that bottles — even one — given in the first two weeks can make successful breastfeeding less likely. After two weeks, we just don't know, as the studies haven't yet been done. However, experienced breastfeeding counsellors and others observe that once breastfeeding is well-established, the occasional or even the regular 'convenience' bottle seems to have less effect.**

Feeding only on breast milk for the first four to six months means that the baby will get the fullest benefits. Your baby will then begin to eat other foods. Remember, any breastfeeding at all is beneficial to your baby.

Q. **Can I start to breastfeed after a period of bottle feeding?**

A. **Yes, but the sooner you switch, the better. In the first days, you produce milk whether or not your baby has come to the breast at all. The milk goes away if the supply isn't stimulated by the baby's sucking, but it can come back if it is stimulated again. This is known as 'relactation'. It is physically possible to relactate, but you need a cooperative baby who is willing to suck, even when there is very little milk.**

There are special breastfeeding aids to help you in this situation which supply formula milk down a tube attached to your nipple, so the baby gets rewarded for sucking. Breastfeeding counsellors, midwives and health visitors can give you more information.

Working and breastfeeding

This is perfectly possible, and many mothers enjoy keeping up the closeness of breast-feeding, even though they are away from their babies while they work. Here are your main options.

- Leave expressed breast milk (EBM — see over the page) for your baby to take from a bottle. To maintain a supply for a fully breastfed baby, you may need to express at work, and keep your milk in the fridge, taking it home in a cool bag.

- Breastfeed your baby when you're together, and leave formula when you are away. Your breasts may fill up at first, and you may need to express at work to keep yourself comfortable, but your body soon adapts. You can even fully breastfeed at weekends, and only half breastfeed in the week.

- Older babies — from about five or six months — can have a cup of EBM (or formula milk), as well as their solids, while you're not there. That way, you don't need to get your baby used to a bottle teat.

Expressing milk

This means removing the milk from your breasts by hand (see picture) or with a special pump (available from chemists or baby stores) — your midwife, health visitor or a breastfeeding counsellor can explain what to do. Electric breast pumps can be hired from breastfeeding support organisations.

feeding

EBM can be stored in the fridge for three to five days, or in the deep freeze for three to six months. Freeze in small quantities — use ice cube trays — to make defrosting easier, and to make the amounts you offer more flexible. Sterilise the container you use. A very rough guide is that younger babies (under three months) take about 100–125 millilitres (ml) per feed (3–4 fluid ounces); older babies take between 150–200 ml (5–7 fluid ounces).

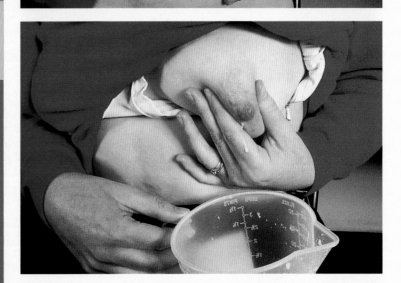

Bottle feeding

Baby formula milk is used instead of breast milk, if a mother doesn't breastfeed. Babies should have only baby formula milk, not ordinary pasteurised cow's milk, until the age of one year (though pasteurised whole cow's milk can be used in cooking from four months).

baby milk

Cow's milk products (eg yoghurts, custard, cheese sauce made with cornflour) can be used in weaning after four months.

Formula milk is usually based on modified cow's milk. Some babies can't take cow's milk at all. Soya milk formula may be prescribed on medical advice for them.

Formula milk is sold in cans, packets or in powdered or granule form, to be mixed with water. Ready-to-feed formula is also sold in cartons. It's more expensive than dried formula.

The protein content of formula milk is based on whey or casein (two different milk proteins). Whey-based formula is usually marketed for babies from birth; casein-based formula is sold for older or hungrier babies. However, both are equally suitable for babies of any age, and there's no real evidence that casein-based formula is more 'satisfying'.

If you are unsure, discuss the issue with your midwife or health visitor.

Q. I changed to using formula milk when my baby was three weeks old. Breastfeeding was such a struggle — every feed left me in tears. He is now so much happier on formula, but I still feel guilty that I didn't breastfeed.

A. Breastfeeding may be the healthiest way to feed a baby, but for you, under stress and upset, it's not necessarily the best way of mothering. However you feed your baby, if he's secure, well-fed and enjoys his feeds, that's great.

It may help you to look back on your breastfeeding experience and understand what went wrong. There's almost always a reason. Perhaps you weren't able to get him on to the breast in a way that got your milk supply off to a good start. Maybe you lacked confidence, or you didn't get the right information and support. Talking it over with a breastfeeding counsellor can help to reassure you. If you have another baby and want to try again, your previous experience will help you avoid problems again. In the meantime, enjoy your baby!

What you'll need to bottle feed

- At least six 200 ml bottles, teats and bottle covers.
- Some way of sterilising your bottles and teats.
- Formula milk.
- Bottle brush.

You can **sterilise** your baby's bottles and teats (and other items such as dummies) in one of four ways:

- in a steam steriliser, which sits on your worktop and plugs in
- in a sterilising unit which you use in the microwave oven
- in a tank you can use with sterilising fluid or tablets (a plastic tub with a lid does just as well)
- by boiling the feeding equipment in a pan for 10 minutes.

If you use sterilising fluid or tablets, rinse the items in cool, boiled water before you use them.

Sterilising removes germs but you must first wash everything thoroughly in hot soapy water. Brush the bottles out and turn the teats inside out to get rid of the obvious remains of milk. Rinse carefully afterwards to get rid of any detergent.

If you have lead plumbing in your house, or leading to your house, see the important note on page 128.

Making up a feed

1. Boil a kettle. Leave the water to cool.

2. Put the measured amount of water in the bottle.

3. Place the correct number of scoops of formula powder or granules in the bottle (level off the scoop — don't pack the milk in). Place the teat and cover on the bottle.

4. Mix by tipping the bottle a few times.

5. Make sure the milk is cool enough before giving it to your baby. The right temperature is when a few drops shaken on to the back of your hand feel slightly warm. You can hurry the process by holding the bottle under a running cold tap.

Note: always get rid of unused milk.

Making up feeds in advance

You can keep bottles in the fridge for 24 hours. Cover the teats with the bottle covers, or leave the teats off, and cover the bottle with the plastic disc that comes with the bottle when you buy it.

Warm the milk by standing it in a jug of hot water, or in a special bottle warmer. Don't use the microwave — it creates random hot spots which could scald your baby's mouth.

Routine care

BATHING, NAPPY CHANGING, CLOTHING

Bathing your baby the first few times can be quite daunting — your baby is so small and wriggly, and it's natural to feel scared you'll do something wrong. You'll become more confident as the weeks go by.

'Top and tail' your baby

A daily or twice-daily 'top and tail' is a quick alternative to a bath for a young baby. You need:

- cotton wool or two soft, clean cloths

- bowl of warm water

- a fresh nappy and clean clothes if necessary

  a bin or bucket for waste.

Wash your hands. Undress your baby on his or her back and leave the nappy on.

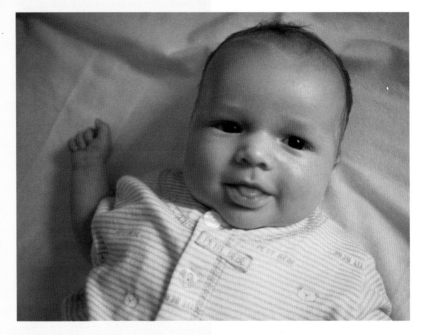

A very new baby may be more comfortable if wrapped in a towel to stay warm.

Wipe your baby's face, neck and ears. Dry with cotton wool or the other cloth, or a towel.

Now wipe the underarms and the hands. Dry.

Take off the nappy. For a new baby, wash any dried discharge that may have come from the cord stump. Wash the bottom and the genitals well. Wipe girls with a clean wet cloth from front to back. Pat dry. Use a protective cream to prevent nappy rash if you wish.

Replace the nappy and dress your baby.

Use plain water, or unscented toiletries made for babies, to keep your baby clean. In the first weeks, most babies don't need anything on their skin. The skin produces its own protection, which can be affected by the use of scented or harsh toiletries.

Q. How do I wash my baby's hair?

A. If your baby doesn't have much hair, you need only rinse the scalp during the bath, pouring some water over it with your hand or a jug. Longer-haired babies may need a tiny drop of mild shampoo on wet hair, lathered and rinsed off. To wash your baby's hair you can support the head and shoulders as he or she lies in the bath, and pour the water over with your other hand. Alternatively, you can wrap your baby in a towel and hold him or her over the bath with one hand, using your other hand to wash.

If your baby has cradle cap — greasy, crusty deposits on the scalp — you can rub in baby or vegetable oil to loosen this, and rinse off.

Bathing

Here's what to do — and all you'll need to know!

- Choose a warm, draught-free room.

- Make sure you have everything you need within reach. **Never leave a baby or a toddler alone in the bath, even for a few seconds, as there is a risk of drowning.** If you need to get something, or answer the phone, take your baby with you, wrapped in a towel.

- Whether you're using a baby bath, or the big bath, put cold water in first and then hot. Test the temperature with your elbow. It should feel comfortably warm.

- Lower your baby into the water, on his or her back, supporting the head and shoulders on your hand and forearm.

- Use your free hand to wet your baby's body and rub over the skin gently with a clean cloth.

- You can use a mild soap or baby bath liquid if you like, but it's not really necessary in the first few weeks.

- Dry your baby in a large absorbent towel and then dress.

Note: you can take your baby into the bath with you, as long as the water isn't too hot. You will need someone to hand you the baby after you get in, and to take the baby from you while you get out.

Nappies

Throw-away nappies are convenient, but expensive compared to washable nappies (even with the cost of washing). They are also hard to get rid of. Green campaigners say they take up space in landfill rubbish sites, take many years to rot down, and are a health hazard if dumped. If you want to use cotton, washable nappies, you can either wash and dry them at home yourself, or use a nappy laundry service, where there is one. The service takes away your dirty nappies and swaps them for clean ones.

Your baby's stools

At first your baby's stools are dark green or blackish, and sticky. This is known as meconium. They change over the first few days to a soft-textured yellow. Bottle-fed babies' stools may be more formed, and a pale brown colour. Some formula milks make the stools greenish. The occasional green stool in a breastfed baby does not matter.

Nappy rash affects many babies. The symptoms are redness or soreness in the nappy area. Dirty nappies should be changed as soon as possible. Clean and dry your baby's bottom carefully to help prevent nappy rash. You can also try leaving your baby to kick without a nappy for short period. Sometimes a rash can get infected, perhaps with thrush. See your health visitor or your doctor.

Clothing — some of the things your child will need

When your baby is young, keep clothing simple with designs that make for easy nappy changing (for example, front-fastening, and poppers up the inside of the legs).

Here's a suggested minimum that will see your baby through the first three months:

- five all-in-one stretchsuits
- five vests
- three cardigans or matinee jackets
- shawl
- bedding for pram — four sheets, two blankets
- bedding for crib/cot — four sheets, two blankets
- hat — warm for winter baby, sunhat for a summer baby
- nappies
- two towels, two washcloths, six cloths (in muslin or soft cotton) for wiping after and between feeds.

After three months, your baby will probably have grown out of some clothes. As he or she moves around more, you will need socks, and an outer garment, since less time will be spent in the cot or pram. The baby will need nightclothes, too, as you will probably develop an evening routine of a bath followed by bed. Bibs are essential when your baby starts solid food — you may need about a dozen.

growing

Toddlers need several sets of clothes, as they dirty their clothes very quickly. Once your child is walking outside, he or she needs shoes. Feet should be measured for length and width, and checked for fitting every three to four months. Good shoe shops won't mind you checking on this, without buying new shoes. Make sure socks fit properly, too.

BABY EQUIPMENT

Later equipment

Most babies grow out of their baby cribs by about three months, so you will need a full-size cot from then on. From about six months, you may need a high chair.

Your child will probably move from a cot to a bed at between two and three years old (see page 117).

Baby slings

These can generally be used from birth (front slings). They allow you to carry your baby close to you, while leaving your hands and arms free. Back packs are designed for older babies who can support their head and neck. You and your partner should try on a few different models before you decide what to buy.

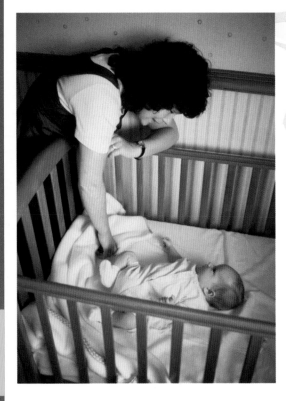

Items for the pram and/or lie-back pushchair

- In a pram, your baby needs one or two layers of lightweight blanket on top in cold weather, waterproof protection from the rain, and a sheet underneath. More layers are needed in a lightweight pushchair, and more if the weather is exceptionally cold. A fabric pushchair, or one which is low to the ground, will be cosier with a blanket underneath your baby as well as on top.

  Don't overheat your baby. If you leave the baby in the pram or pushchair when you come indoors from outside (perhaps because he or she is asleep) take the covers off and any heavy outdoor garments.

- A sun canopy or a parasol is useful in summer, and essential when it's very hot. Make sure your baby is out of the direct sun at all times.

- A shopping tray or basket is handy. The ones that fix underneath won't tip your pushchair over when full, if the baby starts wriggling.

- A safety harness to ensure your child is strapped in. This is not necessary for very young babies who always lie down in the pram or pushchair, but it is essential for older babies and toddlers. You will also need one to fasten your child in the high chair.

Sleeping and crying

SLEEPING PATTERNS, AND WHAT TO DO ABOUT CRYING

New babies only ever sleep for a few hours at a time, and it's normal for them to need feeding in the night. It helps if you can get back to sleep as soon as you can after you have fed your baby. Don't switch on the light, or change your baby's nappy unless you have to. Take your baby into bed to feed so you can relax and your baby stays warm.

Your baby can sleep in a cot or crib next to you for the first months. Later, if you prefer, the cot can be in another room. Some parents sleep better if their baby is in a separate room quite early on. Do what suits you, but if

the baby is close to you, you will hear as she wakes, and can start feeding before she gets upset. Don't worry that you are starting 'bad habits'. It's normal all over the world (and throughout history) for mothers and babies to sleep close to each other.

In daytime, young babies can nap in a pram or carry-cot anywhere in the house. As they get older, they are more likely to be disturbed by noise and activity, and you may find your baby sleeps better in a bedroom.

Babies' sleeping habits change as they grow, but these habits vary widely at all ages. It's not realistic to expect your baby to sleep several times a day, waking only for feeds and happy, smiling, socialising ... a few babies may behave like this, but most don't.

All babies have days when they seem to want to sleep more or are more wakeful than usual. Many babies need more attention in the afternoons and evenings, when they may be irritable and demanding.

A baby who seems unusually sleepy may be unwell.

Cot death — reducing the risk

Cot death, or sudden unexpected death in infancy, claims 50 infants a year in Scotland. It's rare, and we don't yet know what causes it. We do know, however, that there are ways of reducing the risks. Here's how.

- Place your baby on his or her back to sleep.

- Don't smoke during pregnancy or afterwards. If it's not possible to have a smoke-free home, **never** smoke where the baby sleeps. Carers should also not smoke near a baby.

- Place your baby's feet at the foot of the cot, to prevent wriggling down under the blankets and overheating. Make the bed up so that the covers reach no higher than the baby's shoulders.

- Don't allow your baby to become too hot — a good guide is to have the temperature of the sleeping place no warmer than is comfortable for a lightly clothed adult.

- Don't use cot bumpers or a duvet on your baby's cot, and don't wrap the baby up too warmly at night. A vest, a sleepsuit or similar, plus a sheet and one or two covers, depending on the season, is sufficient.

- Take your baby into bed with you if you like, but not if you are a smoker, or if either you or your partner has taken drugs or alcohol.

- Seek medical advice if your baby seems ill with a raised temperature, breathing difficulties or seems less responsive than usual.

- Check your baby often if not in the same room as you.

Older babies and toddlers

Many older babies and toddlers wake in the night. About half of all one year-olds wake up at least once most nights. Many grow out of this by themselves. You may or may not regard it as a problem — for some families, it's just a fact of family life, neither good or bad. They cope, perhaps by sharing a bed with the baby all night, or after she or he wakes.

If it worries you, or you find you are tired and irritable after a broken night, you can try to teach your baby to sleep through (see page opposite).

Children who find it hard to settle to sleep may be helped by a calming evening routine before bedtime. Perhaps a bath followed by a quiet half hour with books or songs. At bedtime, make sure your child is happy and comfortable, and don't prolong the 'goodnight'. Leave a light on if this helps, and if he or she cries, follow the pattern of soothing and calming without fuss suggested in the **Q&A** opposite.

Daytime naps

Most older babies and toddlers sleep at some point in the day until the age of two or three. Some are bad-tempered and irritable if they don't have a nap.

You can encourage a nap at the same time each day (more or less) if you want to. Day nurseries find the children get used to expecting this after a short time, though some babies and toddlers may need help to calm and settle.

Families with toddlers who have trouble settling at night, and in getting back to sleep after waking, are often encouraged to build a nap into the daytime routine. This teaches the child that falling asleep is easy, and prevents the irritable tiredness that makes settling problems worse.

Some children manage perfectly well without a daytime sleep. It's not essential, and may not be what you or your child want.

Q. Can I teach my baby to sleep through?

A. The wakeful baby may not wake up any more often than any other baby. The problem lies in getting back to sleep after waking.

You can change this, though, *if you want to*, after your baby is around seven or eight months old.

When your baby cries, just do what is necessary to settle him or her — then leave. Eventually, your baby will go back to sleep. Don't leave the baby crying for longer than a few minutes. Soothe and calm by talking, cuddling, stroking her back — but leave it at that. Repeat this again and again and again. Don't do anything else — no playing, feeding, and so on. In this way, you can teach your baby to fall back to sleep by herself. This programme may take a week or a fortnight to work, but if you stick at it, it works. You can discuss it with your health visitor.

Q. When should my toddler use a bed instead of a cot?

A. Most babies are in a cot until the age of about two or three, when they simply get too big. If your child learns to climb out of the cot before this time, you may need to make the move sooner, to prevent accidents. If you need the cot for a new baby, leave a few weeks between moving your toddler out of the cot, and the new baby in.

Crying

Some babies cry a lot more than others, and we don't really know why. They are difficult to soothe and seem miserable a lot of the time, although they may be healthy and developing well. If you are worried about your baby's crying, ask your doctor to check them over to reassure you that all is well. If no cause is found, you may just have to accept that this is the way your baby is. It isn't your fault, and you're not doing anything wrong. In time your baby will become happier and more settled.

Some people believe that persistent crying is caused by colic, due to bubbles of wind. If you think this is the cause, you can try medication from your doctor or the chemist, or traditional remedies like gripe water. Follow the instructions on the bottle and give your chosen remedy three or four days to work.

Constant crying in a baby is exhausting and demoralising for you. If you get upset yourself, you may need to put your baby down somewhere safe, or let someone else hold him or her, and leave the room.

It's worth working through a list of possible 'soothers' to help both of you.

- Rocking, patting or gently rubbing your baby's back or tummy.

- Try a baby soother tape, available from large music stores.

- A baby sling, to carry your baby close to you much of the day.

- More frequent breastfeeds — some babies would like 24-hour access if given the chance!

- A dummy, to give your baby sucking comfort.

- A warm bath.

Don't worry about 'spoiling' your baby — you are just offering much needed comfort.

For older babies (from three months) a door bouncer can be hung from the top of a doorway. It has an up-and-down movement which some crying babies love.

If you want to try any complementary therapies, talk to your midwife or health visitor about them.

Always see your doctor if you are concerned about your baby's crying, to check there is no underlying health problem. Get help and support. It can be extremely stressful trying to cope with a baby who seems unhappy. Some parents can become very upset and angry themselves when this goes on for a long time. **Don't ever shake your baby — it can be very dangerous.** See Further help for support groups.

YOUR DEVELOPING CHILD — AT-A-GLANCE PROGRESS

These stages are guidelines only. If you are concerned about your child's development, have a word with your doctor or health visitor.

MONTHS 1–2	MONTHS 3–4	MONTHS 5–6	MONTHS 7–8	MONTHS 9–10
Holds head up for short period of time

Legs less bent when lying on tummy | Kicks vigorously

Keeps head up with little or no support

Lifts head up when placed on tummy with forearms on floor

Back straighter when held in sitting position

From 4 months—starts to take own weight when held in standing position | Sits with support

Rolls front to back

Lying on tummy raises up on palms | Sits unaided

Might shuffle along floor | Might pull self into standing position

May walk anytime between 8–20 months

Can reach out for a toy when sitting without falling over |
| Turns head and eyes towards light | Follows moving object with eyes

Watches own hands | Grasps small objects

Constantly looks around | Loves watching people | Uses index finger to poke small objects |
| Responds to your voice | Turns head to follow sound

Makes noises | 'Speaks' tunefully to self and others | Accurately locates sounds

Babbles and responds with noises

Shows happiness and annoyance | Understands some phrases |
| Begins to smile more | Laughs and chuckles when played with | Puts things in mouth

Plays with feet

Holds arms to be lifted | Drinks out of cup with spout

Can start to eat finger foods (from 6 months) | Copies some sounds and actions (eg coughing, waving)

Stiffens in annoyance |
More awake and alert				
	Less frequent feeds	From 4 months — moving on from milk only		
	May sleep through the night			
Immunisations (from 2 months)		Teething starts at about 6 months		

More over page

YOUR DEVELOPING CHILD — AT-A-GLANCE PROGRESS

MONTHS 11–12	MONTHS 13–18	MONTHS 19–24	YEARS 2–2½	YEARS 2½–3
Walks around furniture and may start walking alone	Walks and can carry larger objects Climbs up and down stairs with adult help	Runs and falls down less often	Runs, climbs and squats easily	Walks up and down stairs Can catch a large ball
Recognises people from some distance Points	May start to show preference for right or left hand Scribbles with crayon	Better manipulative skills	Copies simple shapes with pencil and paper	Distinguishes between some colours Draws recognisable forms
Understands more complex phrases Responds to own name	Holds 'conversations' Tries to repeat words May have between 6–20 words	Uses simple sentences and asks simple questions Responds to simple instructions	Asks questions Tells you stories	Communicates clearly
Shows affection Finds toys hidden in front of his eyes	Feeds self Restless and curious Enjoys putting things in and out of containers	Pretend play Uses own name	Plays with other children	Makes up games Washes hands and face Counts to 10 if taught
			Toilet training	

Months 1–2

EVERY DAY IS DIFFERENT

In the first days after birth, some babies are alert but most babies sleep when they're not feeding. Feeds tend to be short, as the baby often falls asleep or becomes drowsy after a few minutes sucking.

Babies like this will probably be more wakeful after a few days, and will spend longer over feeds. (Some aren't like this — they are alert from the very beginning.) Each day can be different. Your baby feeds and sleeps at unpredictable times without much of a pattern.

As the weeks go on, if things go well, you will become more confident and find it easier to keep your baby contented. Feeding will be easier.

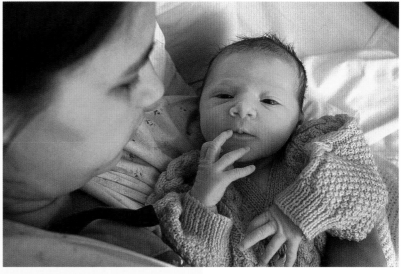

YOUR BABY LEARNS A LOT IN THE FIRST TWO MONTHS

- Hold your baby out in your arms, on his or her tummy, your hands under the chest. By a month your baby will hold his or her head up in line with the body for a short time.

- From five or six weeks your baby 'coos' in response to your voice and attention.

- From the same age your baby begins to smile more often, and stops whimpering to listen to your voice, and turn his or her head towards it.

- If you lie your baby tummy-down, you'll notice that the limbs get less 'tucked in'. A newborn bends the knees and draws them up in a 'frog-like' pose, buttocks humped up. By two months this is much less marked. The legs are bent but less drawn up and the bottom is not as high. (Remember, don't let your baby sleep in this position. Babies should lie on their backs to sleep — see page 116.)

- By two months, your baby will be awake and alert more, and need less frequent feeds. Feeds may take less time, too.

GETTING TO KNOW YOUR HEALTH VISITOR

Your health visitor is a nurse with special training in the health needs, and promotion of good health among families with children under five.

You may meet your health visitor when you are pregnant. About 11 days after the birth of your baby, the health visitor will probably visit you and your baby at home. Your health visitor will tell you about the baby clinic, and when you can bring your baby for immunisations, and talk about progress.

The health visitor's role is to support you, your family and your baby. You can discuss sleep, feeding, weaning, and the baby's development, as well as any aspects of your own feelings and health.

Your child will be offered the first progress check, or routine developmental assessment, at around six to eight weeks. Others are at seven to eight months, at about two, and then shortly before school entry. Your doctor or health visitor will carry them out, either at the clinic or at your home.

At the first check, the assessor will do some basic physical checks, ask you about your baby's progress and answer any questions you may have.

THE CHILD HEALTH CLINIC

You and your baby will be invited to visit the child health clinic. At the clinic, you can ask questions, have your baby's health and growth assessed, and get information about baby care.

Weighing is one useful way of assessing your baby's health. Parents often like to know how their baby is growing. Your health visitor will show you your baby's line on the 'centile' chart. For example, a baby on the 50th centile is average. He or she weighs more than 49 babies of that age out of every 100, and less than another 49 babies of that age out of every 100. There is also a centile chart for length. Weight is only one part of your baby's progress, though. The baby's overall health and development are most important (see also the development chart on pages 119–120).

There may be a doctor at the child health clinic, to give a medical opinion when needed.

Months 3–4

YOUR BABY'S CHANGING

Babies of this age are getting stronger and chubbier. Their faces, arms and legs 'fill out' and any family resemblances become clearer than before.

You can tell your baby recognises you and maybe one or two other familiar faces. The baby knows what to expect from certain routines now, and shows excitement — for instance, when you are getting a bath ready.

Feeds take less and less time, apart from in the evening when it's still quite common for your baby to need a lot of cuddling, feeding and other attention before settling. You can think about beginning an evening routine around now. This may mean you have some time to yourself once your baby is asleep.

A few babies now sleep through the night.

Here's what else your baby is likely to do:

- when placed in a sitting position, keeps the head up, with little or no lag. (Must be supported.)

- when held in a sitting position, the back is straighter than before

- when placed on tummy, lifts his or her head and uses forearms to support the upper body

- be a vigorous kicker, and loves lying on his or her back, having a spot of 'exercise'. May grab a foot and bring it up to the face for a closer look

- when you ring a little bell behind the baby, moving it around, his or her head will turn to follow the sound

- the baby likes a standing position on your lap, and by four months may be starting to take a little of his or her own weight.

PLAYING WITH YOUR BABY

This is the time when babies start to discover just how sociable they can be, and they begin to realise they have an effect on other people. If they respond to your attention, they'll get more of it!

Watch your baby's reactions when you play, and how he or she can now move the 'game' along. Here are some play ideas:

- put a rattle or a small toy in the baby's hands. From about three months babies can hold things, and over the next few weeks hand and eye coordination develops. Your baby will then hold the toy where he or she can study it for a short time

- take your baby to the mirror and look at and talk to 'the baby' in it. Your baby won't realise who this is, but will recognise you. She's not puzzled, though. She just accepts everything

- play with different noises, and see her delight. Try to discover which ones she likes best

- put out your tongue and make funny faces. Your baby may even try to copy you!

- sing songs and hear your baby join in with his own noises

- dangle an object in front of your baby's face. Watch his eyes track its movement from side-to-side and up and down

- sometimes, babies play on their own, studying the shapes their fingers and hands make, moving their blanket to make shadows on the wall, pressing their palms together, waving their hands in front of their face.

Above all, talk to your baby. He or she can't understand your words, but can hear the shapes and sounds of human speech. Your baby is learning all the time about expression, mood and communication.

YOUR BABY'S IMMUNISATIONS

You will be offered three sets of immunisations for your baby in the early months — at two, three and four months of age.

Each time your baby can have:

- the polio vaccine

- a combined vaccine (DTP), against diphtheria, tetanus and pertussis (whooping cough)

- Hib, against Hib meningitis.

Polio vaccine is given as drops which your baby takes by mouth. The other vaccine is given as an injection in the thigh or the buttock.

The **MMR vaccine** protects your child against measles, mumps and rubella. Rubella is also known as German measles. This is usually given in one single injection, usually between 12 and 18 months of age.

The next routine immunisations are between the ages of about three-and-a-half and five, when DT (diphtheria and tetanus) and polio will be given, along with the second dose of MMR.

If you're worried about your baby having any or all of the vaccinations, ask your doctor.

Most doctors agree that the majority of babies should have all the recommended ones. However, if your baby is clearly unwell or running a high temperature when an immunisation is due, tell the doctor and your appointment can be re-scheduled.

Months 5–6

YOUR BABY'S PROGRESS

Your baby may be sleeping through the night at this age, though it is still normal to wake up. Most babies don't actually need a feed when they wake. They may get one, though, as it's certainly a useful way of comforting crying babies and soothing them back to sleep.

Your baby now chuckles and laughs readily when you play together. He or she shows anger by squeaking or screaming suddenly rather than tearful crying. The baby now enjoys watching other babies and children. He or she tries to attract other people's attention by making a noise or waving arms and hands excitedly.

Here are some progress signs during these two months:

- lying on her back, your baby can raise a foot to her face, to play with it, or to suck her toes

- can sit up with support in the pram or on the sofa with cushions around (don't leave her alone like this). Some babies can already sit up by themselves for a few moments

- holds her arms out to be lifted up

- rolls over from front to back and sometimes from back to front

- lying on her tummy, raises her head well up and straightens her arms, with the palms of her hands on the surface

- loves bouncing in a standing position on your lap, or on the floor, while helped to stay 'standing', and takes all her weight on her legs

- can grasp small toys and objects put in front of her, usually using both hands

- if she drops something from the pram she watches it fall. If it disappears, she forgets it quickly, not realising you can look for things and find them again! To her, it doesn't exist any more

- uses her mouth to explore everything

- knows that if she shakes a rattle it makes a noise

- cries or 'crumples' her face if you talk to her crossly

- can pass small objects from hand to hand

- adores rough and tumble play.

MOVING ON FROM MILK ONLY

The word 'weaning' means changing your baby's diet to include foods and drinks other than breast milk or infant formula milk. Sometimes, this is called moving on to 'solids' or 'solid foods' — though at first what you offer your baby may not actually be solid in texture. Babies still taking much of their nourishment from breast or formula are said to be 'on mixed feeding' or on a 'mixed diet'.

The latest Government's report, which looks at the feeding needs of babies and children in the UK, recommends that babies should not have solid foods before four months, and that they should be offered a mixed diet by the age of six months. So, at some point between the ages of four and six months, your baby will need other foods as well as milk.

By this age **(four to six months)** your baby:

- can begin to chew as well as suck

- can swallow food from a spoon, using the tongue to move the food from the front to the back of the mouth

- is curious about other tastes and textures

- is reaching a sociable age and can appreciate the fun of joining in with what other people are doing

- is developing eye-hand coordination which means they start trying to pick things up and put them in their mouth.

First non-milk foods

Very first foods

You don't have to buy anything special. Here are foods suitable for your baby while weaning:

- cooked potato
- baby rice
- cooked swede or turnip
- cooked carrot
- cooked dessert pear, peeled
- cooked dessert apple, peeled
- banana.

Mash, sieve or puree to get rid of lumps. Don't add any seasoning, salt or sugar.

Offer small quantities at first, and only one or two new tastes every few days. A couple of teaspoons at a time may be all your baby will want at first. Once your baby is happily taking a few spoonfuls you can move on to include small amounts of blended meat, chicken, fish (remove bones), or pulses with their meals.

When to offer solids

Once a day is fine at first — before, after or even during your baby's milk feed — do what suits you. Later, you can all begin to share mealtimes. Some of the breast or bottle feeds will start to go, and you can offer a cup from about six months on. Some babies take three months or more to build up to breakfast, lunch and tea; others get there very quickly.

Babies should have begun taking solid foods by the time they reach the age of six months.

A typical menu for a baby of five months

7 am — breastfeed.

8 am — breakfast of baby rice, plus mashed banana.

11 am — drink of plain boiled water.

12 midday — lunch of mashed or sieved potato, carrot and fish. Yoghurt. Breastfeed.

3 pm — breastfeed.

5 pm — tea of chicken, peas and potato (mashed or blended). Drink of water or diluted fruit juice.

7 pm — breastfeed.

These are suggestions only — also, your baby may eat at different times.

Don't avoid lumps and chewy foods for too long. Some babies get so used to smooth textures that they won't eat anything with lumps until well into toddlerhood. Mashing with a fork is sufficient for most foods, even for a baby starting solid food.

LEAD IN DRINKING WATER

If you live in a house with lead pipes or a lead-lined storage cistern, or if your house has a lead pipe leading to it, the water coming into your house may have a high level of lead in it. Although lead in water is no longer a major health problem in Scotland, it is still important to ensure that lead levels in drinking water are kept as low as possible to prevent any effects on the intellectual development of children.

The human body absorbs lead easily from drinking water. Bottle-fed babies, because their intake of water through formula milk is so high, absorb much more than an average adult. And there is evidence that infants retain more lead than adults.

Present levels of exposure to lead in drinking water do not have serious health effects, but can have subtle effects on a child's intellectual development. You will want to ensure your child is not disadvantaged in this way.

You can contact your Environmental Health Department and ask for a sample of your household water to be analysed for the lead levels. (This is a service you may have to pay for.) Water authorities recommend you replace lead pipework and plumbing. Meanwhile, always take water for you or your child from the mains-fed cold tap (usually the tap at your kitchen sink), and always run the mains tap first thing every morning for a minute or two to clear any water in the system that may have been in contact with lead overnight.

For information on vitamin drops for your baby, see page 138.

Months 7–8

TEETHING

By now, most babies have one or two teeth, usually the bottom two incisors (front) teeth. It's quite normal for your baby to have no teeth at all until a year old, and some babies don't get any until after this. You can clean your baby's teeth twice daily with a soft baby toothbrush and a tiny amount of fluoride toothpaste. For more information about caring for your baby's teeth, see page 141.

Does teething cause pain?

There's no real explanation for the way that teething babies can sometimes seem distressed when a tooth is coming through. Why should a perfectly normal happening like teething cause the baby any pain?

For some babies, a day or so's restlessness can ease once a tooth comes through. Babies dribble more, too, at this time, and this can cause soreness on the cheeks and the chin.

Teething gels rubbed on the gums seem to help some babies.

If your baby seems listless and unhappy, don't think these are just teething troubles. It may be illness. Contact your doctor.

SITTING UP, TAKING NOTICE

At this age your baby:

- can sit up unaided for several minutes

- may be able to move along the floor by sliding or shuffling. Some babies are skilled rollers! A few can crawl

- can hold a cup with a spout and drink

- can locate sounds quite accurately, turning the head to the correct side to listen to your voice or to the sound of a toy

- can babble and respond to you with noises.

WHO IS THIS PERSON?

By now, you and your baby have really got to know each other. You can see a real little person who can 'tell' you what she or he likes and dislikes. You may be able to tell if your baby will be placid and easy-going later on, or excitable and needing constant entertainment and fun — quiet and shy, or outgoing and noisy! Like all human beings, your baby may behave differently in some situations and with different people.

YOUR BABY AND OTHER PEOPLE

It's very common for babies to show some degree of wariness or even anxiety towards strangers at around this age. Babies often turn away and bury their face in your shoulder if someone strange tries to talk to them.

Your baby may respond to someone else's approaches, but only when you are there.

For some babies this lasts just a short time; for others, it continues and may get worse. Your baby may hate it if you go out of the room, and you may have to call out to show you are still around. Your baby doesn't yet know that when you are out of sight, you are coming back.

Most babies have other special people in their lives, and they can link certain actions and items with them. Perhaps your baby knows Grandma's house, and recognises it with excitement as you go up the path. The sound of someone's familiar voice may make him or her laugh delightedly, knowing who is coming.

Routines are important at this age, and your baby may not like any change in the pattern of the day. If you go away on holiday, your baby may not feel happy about sleeping in a different cot or room. If nap times are changed, he or she may be grumpy and irritable.

At around seven to eight months your child's hearing and sight will be checked. The child may be given small bricks and you'll be asked about his or her communication skills. Don't be anxious if your child doesn't 'perform' well. If there is any cause for concern, the assessments can be repeated. You'll be asked about your own observations and experience of what your child can and can't do. These, too, are an important and accurate guide to your child's development.

EATING

Finger foods

These are foods your baby can pick up and eat without any help from you. Some babies don't enjoy solids until they're at this stage. Try offering finger foods from six months — they prefer managing themselves instead of being spoonfed.

Cut or slice the foods up into a shape your baby can hold and manoeuvre easily, chewing or gnawing or sucking it. Good finger foods are:

- slices of bread, toast, pitta, nan or chappati
- slices of eating apple, pear
- sticks of carrot, celery, cucumber
- tiny sandwiches with grated cheese, cottage cheese, pure fruit spreads, mashed banana
- savoury cheese biscuits (those without salt)
- fingers of cheese on toast or pizza
- cubes of cheese
- peas (cooked, as a snack)
- cooked pasta shapes — bow shapes or chunky macaroni are easy to pick up
- cooked vegetables.

Note: always stay with your baby when she or he is feeding, in case of choking.

SAFETY AND YOUR CHILD

Being careful about safety begins from your baby's earliest days.

In a car

The baby needs a safe harness in a car seat that's the right size and shape. Legally, babies under a year can travel in the front of a car only if they are in a safety seat, facing away from the traffic. If you have an airbag fitted on the passenger side your baby **must** travel in the back seat.

At home

Many parents are taken by surprise when their baby learns to roll. You turn your back for a few moments, and the baby has moved! Never leave your baby or toddler unattended on a raised surface at any age. He or she may roll off and get hurt.

Look out for:

- trailing flexes from electrical equipment
- open electrical sockets — buy plastic socket covers to block the holes from tiny fingers or block off access to sockets with heavy furniture

- pet paraphernalia — cat litter trays, food bowls, baskets
- hanging tablecloths
- small objects, such as an older child's toys, left on the floor
- hot drinks. **Don't** drink them with a baby on your lap.

Take action

- Fit a smoke alarm preferably on every floor of your home, if you haven't already, and check it is working regularly.
- Know how you and the family can leave your house quickly in an emergency such as a fire.
- Fit fire-guards to open fires or stoves.
- Keep a well-stocked first-aid kit in the kitchen and the bathroom.

- Keep vital numbers (doctor, hospital, partner's work number and so on) by the phone for quick reference by anyone in an emergency.
- Place safety gates at the top and bottom of stairs. Use one across the doorway at times you want your baby to keep out of a room, such as the kitchen. You can still see and 'talk' to each other.
- Don't place objects on the stairs — you could easily trip when carrying your baby, or learner climbers can trip, or harm themselves on the objects.
- Fit safety catches on cupboard doors, low drawers, fridge, freezer — anywhere you store dangerous or messy objects.

Dangers increase when your baby's crawling, cruising round the furniture or walking.

- Keep poisons (including medicines and tablets, bleach, cleaning materials, weedkillers) out of reach and locked away.

- Always place hot liquids, pans, tea and coffee pots and pans well out of reach.

- Turn saucepan handles to the back of the stove and use the back rings whenever possible.

protection

- Apply safety film or fit safety glass on any low level glass surfaces, including doors and tables.

- Fit a guard over the controls of the video and TV.

- Prevent doors slamming shut on your child's fingers by using a door stop. Or tie a cloth across the front and back handles, which stops the door shutting completely.

NEVER leave your child in the bath alone, or alone near any water indoors or out — even a few inches in a bucket is dangerous.

When children are able to talk, teach them their full name. Some two year-olds can manage to say their address, and even their phone number. This can be vital if ever your child gets separated from you in a shopping centre or other busy place.

Sun safety

Always protect babies and toddlers from sunshine. Babies under six months should be kept out of direct sunlight altogether. Keep your child in the shade whenever possible, and use a sunhat or sunshade on the pram or pushchair. If your child is outside on a sunny day, on the beach or in the garden, and crawling or walking, it can be hard to provide shade at all times. Use a child sun-screen cream with a high protection factor (at least 25). Put a T-shirt and hat on your child, and stay indoors in the middle of the day during a British heatwave (or every day if you are holidaying somewhere very hot). Your child will also need more to drink in the heat.

Your health visitor may know of loan schemes which allow you to borrow safety equipment, or hire it for a small charge.

Months 9–10

MOVING AROUND

Most babies can crawl by 10 months, and some can 'cruise' round the furniture. Most can also pull themselves to a standing position with furniture of the right height — but they can't get to the floor again without falling down with a bump.

WHAT ELSE ARE THEY DOING?

Your baby may still be 'clingy'. Babies who haven't gone through this stage may do so now. In somewhere strange, or with new people, they want to stay on your lap, or very near you.

Here are some other skills babies develop at this age. They:

- are quite stable when sitting, and can turn and stretch out to grasp a toy without always toppling over

- can use the index finger to poke at a small object. If they see a hole they try to stick their fingers in it. (Protect electric sockets with special covers.)

- bring their fingers and thumbs together in a pincer movement to pick up something small

- feed themselves quite well with 'finger foods', but cannot yet use a spoon

- babble with recognisable sounds, like 'mamama' and 'dadada', and can imitate some sounds that you make

- love copying funny noises

like raspberries and kissing sounds

- can refuse to cooperate with you, stiffening the body if you want to dress them, and protesting noisily at the same time

- understand phrases like 'no', 'bye bye' and 'dinner'

- watch while you hide a toy under a cloth, and know the toy's still there, triumphantly removing the cloth

- copy your actions to produce an effect. For example, ring a bell, show it to them, give it to them, and they wave it to make the same noise.

PLAYING WITH YOUR BABY

By now, babies are very interested in toys that have some sound, and movement. They can use their fingers and hands to open little doors or to push things along. Show your baby what to do, and enjoyment and curiosity will make him or her copy you.

Babies love examining and handling different objects, and anything easy to hold is fascinating. Check that things are safe, and can't be swallowed. Your baby will enjoy handing you items, and taking them from you as you hand them back.

Put together a busy box for you both to play with together. Talk about the things you're playing with, describe them and say what your baby's doing with them — 'Yes, you're touching that and it's all rough on that side, and this side's smooth ...' Here are some suggestions for your box — you can keep changing the items so there's always something new to study.

- Empty cotton reels.
- Small plastic bottles (throw tops away).
- Scraps of different-textured fabrics.
- Spoons.
- Doll's cup and saucer.
- Wooden bricks.
- Egg cartons.
- Ball.
- Crackly paper.

Babies enjoy **finger games** and **hand games**, like *Round and Round the Garden* and *This Little Piggy*. They learn to look forward to the tickly bit at the end. Your baby may take your hand and make you do it again when you've stopped. Clapping games help your baby's coordination skills. Help your baby to make music, by singing and providing banging and rattling toys to join in with.

Play 'peep-bo' and 'boo', and watch the delight as the baby learns that although you're hiding, you're still there.

Watch how your baby starts games. For example, babies learn that dropping a toy from a high chair means you pick it up ... and if they do it again, you pick it up again, and again, and again!

Your health visitor can help you with some ideas for games if you don't know any, or if you have forgotten them.

Months 11–12

YOUR NEARLY ONE YEAR-OLD

By the end of the first year your baby is showing the first signs of wanting to make decisions, and may get annoyed if you don't agree.

In many ways babies love to cooperate with you. They hold their arms out for their jacket, for example. They often wave 'bye bye' when asked, and try to brush their hair if you give them a hairbrush or comb. They will hand you objects if you ask and offer your hand, and may be able to point to familiar things. But if you say 'Where's Mummy's nose?' they are just as likely to point to their own nose.

Here are some other abilities which show you how far your baby has come in this one year.

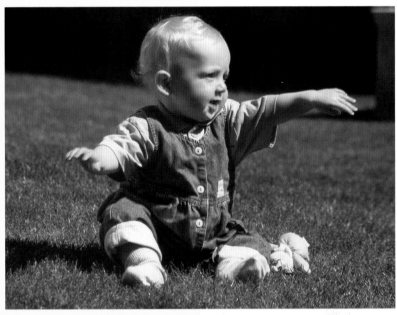

- They can point at an object, so that you'll comment on it, such as, 'Yes, that's a light', 'Yes, you can see a car'. We know they do this to get a response, as babies don't do it when they are alone.

- They may walk at any time from 8 months to 20 months, and some babies may try to climb the stairs (fit stair gates to prevent accidents).

- Non-walkers may bottom shuffle or crawl very quickly, or 'bear walk' using arms and legs extended.

- They can recognise people they know from some distance.

- They know their own name and turn in response to it.

- They understand more complex phrases such as 'Where is the cup?' and 'Do you want a drink?'

- They show affection with cuddles and kisses.

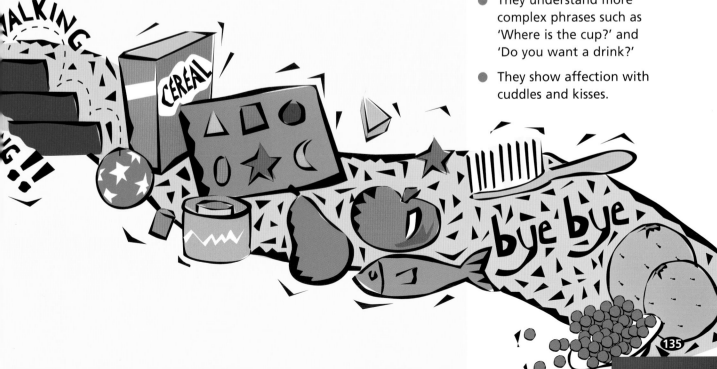

FAMILY MEALS — EATING IN THE SECOND SIX MONTHS

Once your baby is taking a variety of fruit, vegetables and some cereal foods, and showing you enjoyment, think about offering more tastes and textures. Most babies will have three meals a day, and small snacks, by the end of the first year.

When your baby is six months old (or a little older, depending on when you first introduced non-milk foods) you can introduce foods you have been delaying until now.

variety of foods

New foods include:

- cereals containing gluten. Gluten is present in wheat, and in foods containing wheat, including bread and many breakfast cereals, and most flour products (pasta)

- well-cooked eggs from six months

- raw soft fruit and vegetables (lumpier if cooked)

- hard cheese (grated, melted or cubed).

Limit fried foods, and anything very spicy. Don't add salt or sugar to your baby's food.

Avoid nuts. Children who are believed to be sensitive to peanuts should continue to avoid such foods until they are at least three years old, and advice should be taken on obtaining a medical diagnosis. It is also advised that children under five years should not be give whole peanuts because of the risk of choking.

You can use ordinary cow's milk in small amounts in cooking, but until your baby is at least a year old, the best milk for him to drink is breast milk or formula. Tea is not suitable for a baby or toddler — it prevents the absorption of iron.

It's normal for your baby's appetite to vary from day to day, and some babies seem to start eating rather less towards the end of the first year. That's fine, as long as your baby is healthy and happy, and continues to grow, even if the weight gain is a lot slower now.

Ready-prepared baby foods

Most babies will eat ready-prepared, bought baby foods. They're normally made without added salt or artificial additives. They're also convenient to use and are a useful stand-by.

However, your baby doesn't need to have any bought baby foods — and they are certainly no better than freshly-prepared home-cooked foods. Preparing your own food may take a little longer, but it's definitely worth making sure your baby has regular chances to experience the variety of textures and tastes in homemade food. Some babies who have a lot of baby foods may not want to try the 'real' stuff, and some actually gag on the lumps and 'bits' in it. It may take a lot of patience to get them to enjoy family meals.

The nutritional content of ready-prepared foods is worth considering. Added sugars make baby foods, desserts in particular, very sweet indeed. Many baby foods have a high water content, and this means they need starchy thickeners as a result. While these thickeners may do no harm, they are low in food value, and don't represent good value for money either.

Read the labels on baby foods, to avoid the highly-sweetened varieties, and the ones with a high water and starch content. Thickeners are labelled as vegetable gum, gelatine, modified starch and different types of flour. You may also see the term 'maltodextrin'. This is a starch-based bulking agent of little nutritional value.

As with pre-prepared foods for adults, the main ingredient is listed first on the label. You'll find you pay more for better quality baby foods, with a low water and starch content.

questions answered

Q. When should my baby use a cup?

A. Start introducing a cup at any time from six months. Your baby will need help at first.

Q. When should my baby stop breastfeeding?

A. There are no nutritional reasons for stopping in the first year. Worldwide, many mothers breastfeed for a lot longer, and breast milk is always a healthy drink, whatever your baby's age. When your baby is taking to solids, and is learning to take fluids from a cup, then you may want to cut down breastfeeding — perhaps to go back to work, or simply because you want to move on from this stage.

Q. And what about bottles?

A. Bottles are different. A baby still taking several bottles of milk a day could well be filling up with milk, and not getting vital nutrients from other foods. Aim to phase out your baby's bottles by the age of a year or so, apart from perhaps a bedtime one (don't let your baby sleep with it in his or her mouth). If your baby is very keen on bottles, do this gradually, offering a cup with meals, and taking a cup when you go out visiting.

Here's a typical day's eating for a baby of around 11 months.

7 am: milk drink or breast/bottle.

8 am: breakfast of scrambled egg, toast, diluted fruit juice.

10 am: mid-morning milk drink.

12 midday: lunch of lamb and mashed carrot and potato, satsuma, diluted fruit juice or water.

3 pm: drink, toast, scone or breadstick.

5 pm: tea of yoghurt, cracker, portion of mashed banana, milk drink.

7pm: bedtime breast/ bottle.

These are suggestions only — also, your baby may eat at different times.

questions Q&A answered

Q. **Is a vegetarian diet enough for a baby?**

A. **Yes. Your baby does not need meat or fish to stay healthy. Vegetarian babies can get the necessary protein and other nutrients from other parts of their diet — pulses, eggs, milk, grains and cereals.**

A vegan diet — which excludes animal products like eggs and milk — can be healthy for a baby, too, but there is a risk that the diet may not include enough of certain nutrients. It is a good idea to speak to a dietitian if you are thinking of weaning your baby onto a vegan diet. Speak to your health visitor or GP to arrange this. For more information you can write to the address on page 155.

For more information about healthy eating, see page 13.

What about vitamin drops?

Your health visitor or GP will give you advice on infant vitamin supplements. They are usually given to babies as liquid drops. The current official advice is that bottle-fed babies over six months who take less than 500 ml of formula a day (less than a pint) need vitamin supplements. Breastfed infants should start vitamin supplements at six months.

Babies and children over a year on a varied diet may not need supplements.

Months 13–18

BECOMING A TODDLER

Most children learn to walk during these months, though a few may be 'bottom shuffling' or 'bear walking' so well that they don't try to walk properly until later. Children can now walk and carry one or two large toys at the same time without losing their balance. They can walk up and down stairs with adult help. By the end of this period they can climb into a full-size chair, or squat on the floor to play or to pick something up.

Children can control their hands and fingers, and build a small tower of three bricks, if you show them what to do. They may now show a preference for the left or the right hand — watch which one they use when you offer crayons or pencils.

At mealtimes, they use a spoon fairly well. They are much less likely to explore every object they pick up with the mouth. They love to

explore — knobs, cupboards and drawers fascinate them. They want to see behind doors. This is the start of a period that can be quite physically exhausting for you — you seem to be running round after your child all day, and needing eyes in the back of your head!

Understanding and communication skills grow a great deal in this time. Children can:

- put things in and out of a container, and play with a simple shape sorter after practice

- use anything between 6 and 20 words in 'conversation'

- repeat words or try to do so when asked

- try to sing and to join in with songs

- learn 'party tricks' such as telling you what the dog says, or what the cow says

- talk to themselves, while playing. You may hear your child say 'No' when about to do something he or she knows you won't approve of.

Books and your baby

You can introduce books to your baby from the very first weeks. Start by enrolling your baby in your local library, and by buying some books he or she can look at on your lap.

Books for your baby can be any size and shape. Babies seem to prefer small, strong, sturdy books, with pages that can be turned easily.

stories & pictures

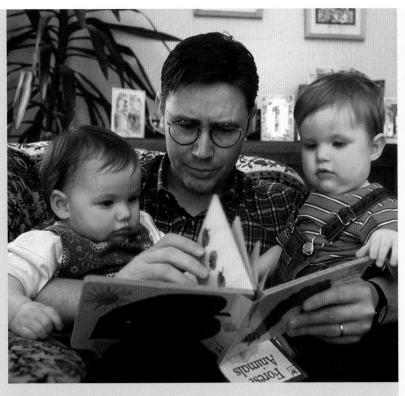

From about six months, your baby learns to anticipate, and to pick up clues that something familiar is about to happen. Babies enjoy books where they know what's going to be on the next page. They can learn from this. A book where a baby gets dressed, with a new garment put on on each page, is a 'story' that's just right for a baby from about nine months.

When you show and talk about these books to your baby, relate the pictures to his or her own life and routine. When the book baby has socks on, for example, show your baby his or her socks. When you see a face, point to the nose, eyes and mouth and so on, and then point out your baby's, and your own, nose and eyes and mouth.

Have some paper books you don't mind your baby messing up — old mail order catalogues are wonderful for babies —

they love the sections with the babies in. Make your own scrap books for your baby to look at, and put in pictures you know are special and relevant. Include a few photos of friends and family, and the baby. If your baby gets excited at dogs, or cats, or cars, have lots of pictures of these.

YOUR CHILD'S TEETH

Start good habits by:

- brushing your baby's teeth as soon as they appear — or rub them with a clean cloth if there are only one or two

- using only a tiny amount of fluoride toothpaste — about the size of a pea

- avoiding giving your baby sugary snacks and drinks between meals, and keep high sugar foods to a minimum

- giving water to drink, or if you give fruit juice, dilute it with water (1:10) and don't offer sweet drinks in bottles.

Register your baby with a dentist at any time from six months, or when the first tooth comes through and take them along for visit. Ask your dentist about fluoride supplements.

Iron

Research shows that some babies and toddlers in the UK don't get enough iron in the foods they eat.

This important mineral is essential for health and development. Some children who are short of iron are listless, lacking in energy and have a poor appetite. However, others appear happy and healthy, and the deficiency isn't diagnosed.

Iron is found in red meat, eggs, cereals, pulses, dried fruits and some vegetables. Your child needs more iron from about four months. Breast milk and infant formula supply some of the iron, but your child needs it from other sources, too.

Make sure your child has enough iron

- In the first year, give your child breast milk or infant formula as a drink, rather than cow's milk (whole pasteurised milk) which is comparatively low in iron. The iron in breast milk is absorbed better if breastfeeds are given separate from solid food.

- Offer at least one serving per day of a food containing iron from the age of six months.

- Serve foods containing Vitamin C. Vitamin C helps the body to absorb iron, and is found in fruits and vegetables (raw or lightly cooked to preserve the Vitamin C content).

Don't give your child tea to drink. It reduces the absorption of iron in the gut.

Months 19–24

LEAVING BABYHOOD BEHIND

By the end of this period, children can run, and they fall down much less often. They can propel themselves forward (and often backwards as well) on a small trike, but very few children can use the pedals yet. They attempt to kick a large ball, by walking into it and then kicking their feet out.

During this time, climbing and 'acrobatic' skills develop. Children will now use imagination when trying to get something that's out of reach — pulling a chair or a table across to use it as a platform. They can show concentration, and their hands are steady enough to build a tower of six or seven small bricks. Their manipulative skills show — they can turn the pages of a book one at a time, and unwrap a sweet.

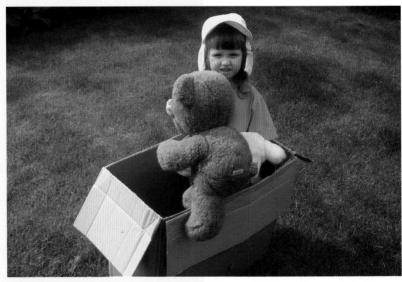

Children enjoy copying people, and by two, they like pretend play with, say, dolls, teddies or cars. They show determination and anger when stopped from doing something they want to do. They may not like sharing toys. They can be very demanding about getting attention. They enjoy the company of other children, but still can't play with them in any meaningful way, and may show aggression towards them. Tantrums and displays of temper are very common.

Your child may show great progress in speaking, talking and listening, and can:

- put two words together, sometimes three or more, to make a simple sentence ('Mummy, Mummy ... go home now?')

- ask questions about the surroundings ('What's that?')

- know his or her own name and use it

- respond to easy instructions, such as 'Go and get the dog's lead'.

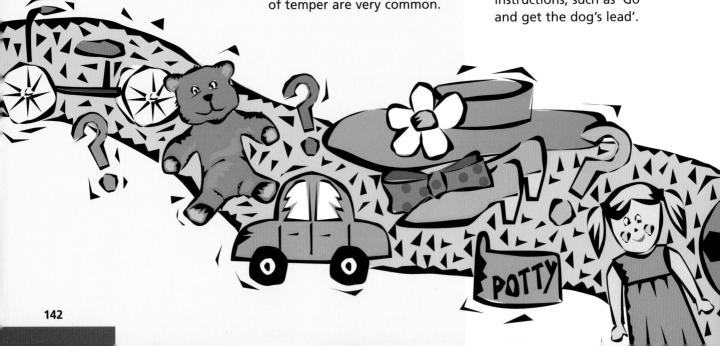

TOILET TRAINING YOUR CHILD

You can start teaching your child about bladder and bowel control at some time around the second birthday, though for some children, this is too soon. Children are usually ready for learning about it when they:

- understand simple commands like 'Put your shoes on the floor'

- go for a couple of hours without a wet nappy

- manage to help you when getting dressed and undressed

- know when they have opened their bowels or bladder.

If your child is at this stage, and you don't have any other major events going on in your family at present (like a house move, a holiday or a very new baby), then you can try training.

Tell your child what you are planning to do, and if you can, show him or her what other children do. Visit the toilet together, and explain what you are doing in a way he or she can understand.

Here's some suggestions you can follow.

- If you recognise when your child needs to open his bowels, sit him or her on the potty. If the child manages to do something, give lots of praise. If not, just be casual about it.

- If you have a couple of hours or more at home, with your child, don't put on a nappy. Every so often, see if the child will sit on the potty. You may be able to prolong the time spent there by looking at a book together. Again, if something happens, give praise and encouragement.

- Increase the opportunities to use the potty or the toilet, and offer occasional reminders about it.

It helps if you:

- have a potty downstairs and upstairs, for quick access

- have spare pants and a bag for the wet ones when you go out.

Accidents will happen. Almost all toddlers will wet or soil themselves many times before they are reliably trained. If your child wets or soils several times a day, it may be too soon for training. There is no shame in going back to nappies, and it may be much less stressful. Stay calm when your child has an accident. Simply clean up, and tell your child it doesn't matter.

Disposable trainer pants are sometimes helpful for this in-between stage. They absorb 'the accident' so it doesn't go through to the outer clothing, yet they can be pulled up and down like normal pants for use with the potty or toilet. However, not all parents like them — some feel they are too much like a nappy, and confuse the not-quite-trained child.

For more information about toilet training, see page 145.

2 – 2½ years

YOUR SOCIABLE CHILD

Now your child begins to be more sociable with other children, playing games where he or she has to take a turn, without protesting or just not understanding.

Your child may be able to manage her or his clothing when using the potty or toilet, but probably needs help. A few children are dry at night.

Your child now has confidence in physical skills, and the energy for running around in open, safe spaces. She or he can copy simple shapes and even letters made up of straight lines (like T or L) with a pencil and paper.

The child can drink from a cup without a lid, and use a fork. Spoon-feeding himself or herself is easy.

Your child's language is more sophisticated, and understandable to people outside the immediate family circle. There will still be difficulty with some sounds, and pronouns (she, me, you, I and so on) may still confuse him.

At this stage, children:

- use 200 or more recognisable words and build sentences

- know their full name, and possibly address or town (if you teach this)

- ask questions with words like 'Why' and 'Who'

- can fill in the missing word when you read from a familiar story book, or sing a song she or he knows well

- can tell you of events that have happened and/or are about to happen.

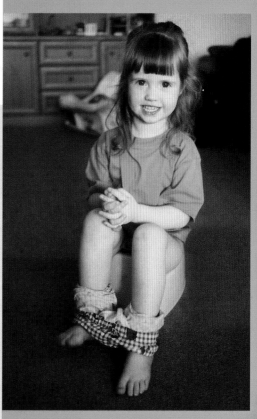

MORE ON TOILET TRAINING

Toddlers of two-and-a-half or so who haven't yet used the potty may be able to skip the potty stage altogether. They may be big enough to get on the toilet with help. A toddler seat can give extra comfort and security at first. It helps if you encourage your child to use a toilet from the start, at least from time to time, to avoid having to take a potty with you everywhere you go.

Before the age of about two-and-a-half, most children are not able to 'hang on' more than a very short time when they want to use the toilet.

2½ – 3 years

YOUR ACTIVE CHILD

By the end of three years, your child is agile, energetic and confident, and moves efficiently. He or she can walk upstairs and downstairs with alternating feet (when coming downstairs, children usually jump from the bottom step, with two feet together). She or he can stand on tiptoe and walk in this way, and stand on one foot without wobbling over straight away.

If you throw a large ball, your child can catch it, usually on or between the arms, rather than with the hands. He or she can ride a trike using the pedals.

Now your child can use a pencil to draw a recognisable human form, with a head, arms and legs, or other features. He or she begins to know colours. Red and yellow usually come first, and it may take longer to tell blue from green.

Most children are able to dress and undress themselves, at least partially, if their clothing is simple. They can wash their hands and face, though they may need help with proper drying.

They can start to share, and they join in pretend play with other children, often making up quite elaborate games with playthings.

They can communicate with family and others well and clearly, and enjoy keeping a conversation going.

- They can count to 10 if taught, but don't really understand the concept of numbers beyond two or three.

- They know several nursery rhymes by heart.

- They can tell you how old they are.

- They use pronouns correctly and pronounce more accurately.

Q. How can I teach my child to be dry at night?

A. Night-time dryness usually comes after daytime dryness. While most children achieve this at about three, it's common for some to be wet at night until five or six or more. Wait until you have a few dry night nappies, and then leave them off, telling your child what you are doing and why. Make it easy for your child to go to the toilet at night. If you decide to take your child to the toilet at night, make sure you wake him or her. Otherwise you are teaching them to urinate in their sleep, which is exactly what you don't want to happen.

Night-time wetting is not usually considered a problem until the age of about seven, as so many children simply grow out of it.

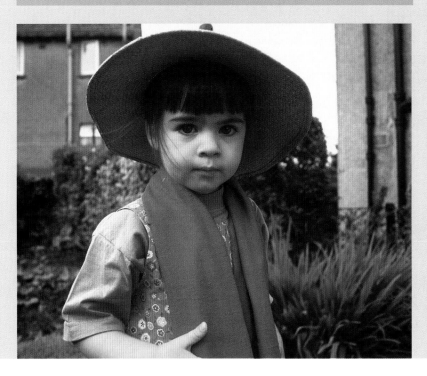

HEALTHY EATING FOR YOUR CHILD

Toddlers need foods from all the different food groups (see page 13), but their need for energy-rich foods is higher than an adult's. Toddlers can't eat a large amount of food at any single meal, they prefer small meals with snacks between them.

healthy food

A good, healthy diet for your child will include vegetables, fruit, bread, cereals and grains (rice, pasta, breakfast cereals), meat and fish, milk, eggs, dairy products (cheese, fromage frais, yoghurt).

If your child has a good appetite you can introduce semi-skimmed milk from age two.

If your child is vegetarian, pulses (lentils and beans) and soya foods will be needed to replace the meat and fish (otherwise the rest is the same). Keep sweetened and sugary foods to a minimum, and continue to follow the advice on dental health on page 141.

Eating problems

Eating problems are common in the toddler years. There are times when children seem to eat a lot more, or a lot less, than at other times. They may 'go off' foods they've always liked, or develop favourite foods which they used to reject.

This is all very natural — children have likes and dislikes, just as you do. They are developing their independence, and want to make choices. They want to choose what they eat just as they want to make decisions over other things in their daily life.

With some children, their developing preferences can spring from a different source — it's as if they want the familiar and the 'safe', in a world which is still, in part, a bewildering collection of different and unexpected events and activities.

Parents worry that these eating habits can lead to poor nutrition. It's also annoying to have a child whose behaviour at the table is upsetting and who continually says 'No' or who has to be persuaded all the time to eat things.

However, making a fuss over your toddler's eating habits risks making them more difficult to handle. Here are some ideas to help:

- offer your child small quantities, cut up into bite-sized pieces
- offer gentle encouragement and praise when he or she eats
- if food is rejected or only a few mouthfuls eaten, accept the child's 'verdict' and remove the plate
- always have something to eat when your child eats, to make the mealtime a social occasion. This will also help to divert your attention from his or her plate
- let the child feed herself
- never force feed
- don't make food into a disciplinary issue (like saying 'It's naughty to leave your dinner' or making threats)
- have your child weighed to reassure you about growth
- don't allow filling up on milk between meals
- snacks are fine, but don't give anything too substantial too close to a meal
- if your child asks for something an hour after a rejected dinner, don't make a fuss. Provide something — but don't make snacks generally more appealing than the meal
- don't talk about your child's eating habits in front of her or him.

Sometimes, problems do get worse, and a child's health suffers as a result. They may not get all the nutrients they require.

A child may not gain weight satisfactorily, or stick to such a limited diet of sweetened foods that teeth are affected.

These effects are rare, but they need to be checked for. Your health visitor or doctor can arrange for a full health check and perhaps a consultation with a dietitian.

Remember, even very young children can be moody — don't worry unduly and remember to always seek advice and reassurance from your health visitor.

Illness and what to watch out for

Babies and small children can't tell you when they aren't well — it's up to you to decide whether your child is feeling ill, and how seriously to take it.

Most babies will have some 'off days' in their first year — mild feverishness can bring a few bouts of irritable, restless crying. Occasionally, symptoms are not mild, and you need to get help. Sometimes you're worried about puzzling symptoms, and you need to know from your doctor whether there is anything seriously wrong. Mild illnesses such as coughs or colds are common. They can be worrying for you, so do seek advice if you are concerned. Severe, life-threatening illness is very rare in babies and young children.

See your doctor (or speak on the phone) if your baby:

- seems listless, or much less alert than usual, or sleeps for an unusually long time

- has continuous vomiting which lasts more than an hour

- has diarrhoea which doesn't clear up in a day

- has a rash which you can't explain by it being a heat rash or a result of clothes rubbing

- has dry nappies

- passes stools which are an unusual colour or texture for him or her (green stools from time to time are nothing significant, and some baby formulas result in green stools routinely)

- seems feverish and uncomfortably hot (check the chest rather than the forehead — if the skin feels sweaty and hot, the child probably has a temperature)

- has unexplained bruising or bleeding from the ears, mouth, nose, anus or in the stools or the urine.

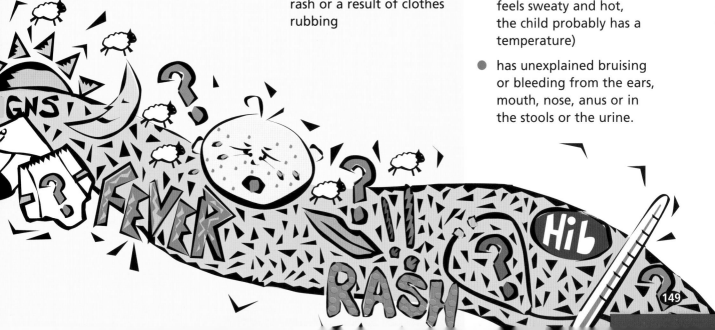

Seek medical help straight away if your baby:

- has a convulsion — continuous twitching or jerking with unfocused, rolling eyes and a lack of response
- has breathing difficulties
- loses consciousness
- becomes blue around or on the lips or the face
- has symptoms of suspected meningitis (see opposite)
- passes blood or redcurrant-jelly-like stools
- seems in obvious pain.

Although babies who scream for a long time are very worrying to parents, babies who are really ill don't cry continuously and loudly. If your baby is making such a noise, he or she is basically okay, though of course may be in distress or uncomfortable. Constant whimpering and moaning is more likely in a baby who is poorly.

For more information on crying see page 118.

Your doctor may not always prescribe medication for your baby — sometimes it's not appropriate, as your baby doesn't need it.

MENINGITIS AND SEPTICAEMIA — WHAT TO LOOK FOR

Meningitis is an inflammation of the meninges, the protective membranes covering the brain and spinal cord. Different forms are caused by bacteria, and by viruses. Meningitis is rare, but can be a very serious illness. If it's diagnosed and treated early, the majority of children make a full recovery.

Septicaemia — blood poisoning — is caused by the same bacteria which causes most cases of meningitis but is the far more life-threatening form of the disease.

The Hib vaccine protects against Hib meningitis only, and no other forms. There are vaccines against some of the other forms of meningitis, and if these have been identified in a sufferer, other members of the family can be offered vaccination.

If your child appears ill, look for these signs:

In babies

- high temperature
- refusing feeds
- fretfulness
- vomiting

- high-pitched, moaning cry
- turning away from light
- staring or trance-like expression
- sleepiness, and being difficult to wake
- pale, blotchy skin or a rash of tiny spots
- bulging fontanelle (the soft spot on the skull).

In toddlers and older children

- high temperature
- vomiting
- pains in the joints
- headache
- dislike of bright light
- neck stiffness
- drowsiness, confusion
- rash of red/purple spots or bruises which will not fade under pressure of a glass tumbler.

For more information on meningitis and septicaemia, see the Further help section at the back of this book.

TRUST YOUR INSTINCTS. IF YOU THINK YOUR BABY IS ILL, GET HELP

Further help, information and useful addresses

The following organisations may be able to put you in touch with local sources of help in your area. Those outwith Scotland may have details of Scottish contacts. Call them for assistance and a friendly chat. Many of them provide helpful leaflets on request. Where they exist telephone helpline numbers have been included – you may wish to contact them for helpful advice, counselling or simply for general information.

A very useful service which provides information about where to find help is available locally through your local health education/promotion unit which is listed under 'Health' in your phone book and/or **The NHS Helpline Tel: 0800 22 44 88** (all calls free of charge; open 9am to 8pm Monday to Friday). Your public library is also an invaluable source of information.

For further information about any health-related issues, please contact:

Health Promotion Library Scotland, The Priory, Canaan Lane Edinburgh EH10 4SG

Tel: 0645 125 442
Textphone: 0131-536 5593

ABUSE

Children 1st (formerly the Royal Scottish Society for Prevention of Cruelty to Children) Melville House, 41 Polwarth Terrace Edinburgh EH11 1NU
Tel: 0131-337 8539
e-mail: children1st@zetnet.co.uk
Offers practical help to families with children at risk.

Parentline Endway House, The Endway Hadleigh, Essex SS7 2AN
Helpline: 01702 559900
Confidential and anonymous telephone helpline run by volunteers for parents/carers.

Parents Anonymous 6-9 Manor Gardens, London N7 6LA
Tel: 0171-263 8918
Telephone helpline run by volunteers for parents under stress who feel they can't cope or might abuse their children.

Scottish Women's Aid 12 Torphichen Street Edinburgh EH3 8JQ
Tel: 0131-475 2372
e-mail: scowomaid@atlas.co.uk
Advice, support and refuge to women who have been abused mentally, physically or sexually, and their children.

ACCIDENT PREVENTION & SAFETY

British Red Cross Society (Scottish Region) Alexandra House, 204 Bath Street Glasgow G2 4HL
Tel: 0141-332 9591
Provides a range of caring and first-aid services and courses.

Child Accident Prevention Trust (CAPT) 18-20 Farringdon Lane London EC1R 3AU
Tel: 0171-608 3828
e-mail: safe@capt.demon.co.uk
Offers help and advice to parents on the prevention of childhood accidents.

The Royal Society for the Prevention of Accidents (RoSPA) Slateford House, 53 Lanark Road Edinburgh EH14 1TL
Tel: 0131-455 7457
Information and advice on the prevention of accidents of all kinds.

St Andrew's Ambulance Association St Andrew's House 48 Milton Street, Glasgow G4 0HR
Tel: 0141-332 4031
Provides training in first-aid and related subjects.

ADOPTION

Scottish Adoption Association 2 Commercial Street Edinburgh EH6 6JA
Tel: 0131-553 5060
Offers a comprehensive adoption service including advice and counselling to anyone affected by adoption.

ALCOHOL, DRUGS AND SMOKING

Alcoholics Anonymous (AA) 50 Wellington Street Glasgow G2 6HJ
Tel: 0141-226 2214
Helpline: 0345 697 555
Network of self-help groups where members encourage each other to stop drinking and to stay off drink. Look in the phone book for details of your local group.

Scottish Council on Alcohol (SCA) 2nd Floor, 166 Buchanan Street Glasgow G1 2NH
Tel: 0141-333 9677
e-mail: sca@clara.net
Provides free, confidential counselling services for people affected by alcohol problems. Promotes safer, healthier drinking styles, but is not anti-alcohol.

National Drugs Helpline 0800 77 66 00
Free 24-hour confidential drug information, advice and counselling service.

Scottish Drugs Forum Shaftesbury House 5 Waterloo Street, Glasgow G2 6AY
Tel: 0141-221 1175 (24 hours)
Offers information on local treatment and services for drug users, family and friends.

ASH Scotland 8 Frederick Street, Edinburgh EH2 2HB
Tel: 0131-225 4725
e-mail: ashscotland@dial.pipex.com
Information and resources to encourage smokers to quit.

Smokeline 0800 84 84 84
Scottish national helpline for smokers who need advice or help in stopping, or their friends who are encouraging them to stop. Staffed by trained counsellors who can send you a free copy of a helpful guide.

BEHAVIOURAL DIFFICULTIES

Hyperactive Children's Support Group 71 Whyke Lane, Chichester PO19 2LD
Tel: 01903 725182
Answerphone: 01903 734726
Web site: http://ourworld.com-puserve.com/home pages.enuresis
Provides information and ideas to parents and professionals about nutritional/dietary therapies for hyperactive and allergic children.

BREASTFEEDING

The Breastfeeding Network P.O. Box 11126, Paisley PA2 8YB
Offers independent information and support about breastfeeding.

La Leche League (Great Britain) BM 3424, London WC1N 3XX
Tel: 0171-242 1278
(24-hour answerphone/helpline)
Help and information for women wanting to breastfeed their babies and personal counselling to mothers having problems in breastfeeding. Local groups hold friendly, informal discussions on breastfeeding, birth and parenthood.

The National Childbirth Trust Alexandra House, Oldham Terrace Acton, London W3 6NH
Tel: 0181-992 8637
Help and information for women wanting to breastfeed their babies. Breastfeeding counsellors can offer personal support.

CHILDCARE

Daycare Trust/National Childcare Campaign Wesley House, 4 Wild Court London WC2B 4AU
Tel: 0171-405 5617
Information and advice on obtaining suitable forms of childcare and on setting up daycare.

**National Association of Toy &
Leisure Libraries/Play Matters
10 Suffolk Road
Edinburgh EH16 5NR
Tel: 0131-662 4454**
Toy Libraries loan good quality, carefully chosen toys to all families with babies and young children, including those with special needs.

**Parents at Work
5th Floor, 45 Beech Street
Barbican, London EC2Y 8AD
Tel: 0171-628 3565
Helpline: 0171-628 3578**
Campaigns to improve the quality of life for working parents and their children; provides practical information about childcare options, ways of balancing work and home, and employment rights.

**Scottish Childminding Association
Room 7, Stirling Business Centre
Wellgreen, Stirling FK8 2DZ
Tel: 01786 445377
Advice line: 01786 449063**
Works to promote high quality daycare for children under eight years and provides help and advice for childminders and parents.

**Scottish Pre-school Play Association
14 Elliot Place, Glasgow G3 8EP
Tel: 0141-221 4148**
Organisation for playgroups, mother-and-toddler groups, and under-five groups in Scotland.

**Working for Childcare
77 Holloway Road, London N7 8JZ
Tel: 0171-700 0281**
Advice and information for employers, trade unions and parents on developing childcare at work.

DISABILITY AND ILLNESS (GENERAL SUPPORT)

**Action for Sick Children
15 Smith's Place
Edinburgh EH6 8HT
Tel: 0131-553 6553**
Supports sick children and their families. Offers information about going to hospital designed for children and for parents. Hospital playboxes available for borrowing by playgroups.

**Association of Parents of Vaccine
Damaged Children
21 Saughton Mains Gardens
Edinburgh EH11 3QG
Tel: 0131-443 9287**
Concerned with obtaining adequate compensation for children damaged by vaccination; also offers support to families.

**Contact A Family (CAF)
170 Tottenham Court Road
London W1P 0HA
Tel: 0171-383 3555
e-mail: info@cafamily.org.uk**
Encourages mutual support between families caring for children with any type of disability or special need.

**Disability Information Scotland
Disability Helpline: 01506 433468**

**Disability Information Trust
Mary Marlborough Centre
Nuffield Orthopaedic Centre
Headington, Oxford OX3 7LD
Tel: 01865 227592
e-mail: disinfo@sable.ox.ac.uk**
Assesses and tests equipment for people with disabilities.

**Disability Scotland
Princes House, 5 Shandwick Place
Edinburgh EH2 4RG
Tel: 0131-229 8632
Minicom service**
Information and advice on all aspects of disability: access and mobility, equipment, community care and daily living problems.

**ENABLE
6th Floor, 7 Buchanan Street
Glasgow G1 3HL
Tel: 0141-226 4541
Freephone: 0800 026 4444
e-mail: enable.org.uk**
Promotes the rights and needs of people with learning disabilities and their families. Can offer information, advice and practical help.

**Family Fund Trust
P.O. Box 50, York YO1 2ZX
Tel: 01904 621115
Textphone: 01904 658085**
Government-funded Trust whose purpose is to ease the stress on families who care for severely disabled children under 16 by providing grants and information related to the care of the child.

**Genetic Interest Group (GIG)
Farringdon Point
29-35 Farringdon Road
London EC1M 3JB
Tel: 0171-430 0090
(24-hour answerphone)**
Information service for people with or at risk of genetic conditions.

DISABILITY AND ILLNESS (SPECIALISED SUPPORT)

**AFASIC
Overcoming Speech Impairments
347 Central Markets
London EC1A 9NH
Tel: 0171-236 3632**
Provides advice and information on speech and language difficulties amongst children.

**Association for Children
with Heart Disorders
Killieard House, Killicrankie
Perthshire PH16 5LN
Tel: 01796 473204**
Provides support to children and young adults with heart disorders, and their families.

**British Diabetic Association (BDA)
34 West George Street
Glasgow G2 1DA
Tel: 0141-332 2700
e-mail: scotland@diabetes.org.uk**
Provides practical help and information on living with diabetes.

**Capability Scotland
11 Ellersly Road
Edinburgh EH12 6HY
Tel: 0131-313 5510
e-mail: cs.ascs.commercial@virgin
Web site: http://www.capability-scotland.org.uk**
Offers advice, support and information to parents of children with cerebral palsy.

**Child Growth Foundation
2 Mayfield Avenue
Chiswick, London W4 1PW
Tel: 0181-994 7625/995 0257
e-mail: cgflondon@aol.com**

Support group for parents of children with growth disorders, and parents concerned about their child's growth.

**Cleft Lip and Palate Association
(CLAPA)
CLAPA Head Office
134 Buckingham Palace Road
London SW1W 9SA
Tel: 0171-824 8110 (24 hours)
e-mail: clapa@mcmail.com**
Offers support to parents of children with cleft lip and/or palate. Offers a specialist service to those seeking help in feeding babies with clefts.

**The Coeliac Society
P.O. Box 220, High Wycombe
Buckinghamshire HP11 2HY
Tel: 01494 437278**
Advice and information for those with the coeliac condition or dermatitis herpetiformis.

**Craighalbert Centre
The Scottish Centre for Children
with Motor Impairments
1 Craighalbert Way
Cumbernauld G68 0LS
Tel: 0236 456100**
Scottish national centre which offers a system of 'conductive education' which aims to teach the cerebral palsied child all aspects of daily life, develop learning ability and prepare the child for school.

**Cystic Fibrosis (CF) Trust
Princes House, 5 Shandwick Place
Edinburgh EH2 4RG
Tel: 0131-221 1110**
Through its Family and Adult Support Service, offers emotional, practical and financial support to people with CF and their families.

**Haemophilia Society
3rd Floor, Chesterfield House
385 Euston Road
London NW1 3AU
Tel: 0171-380 0600
(24-hour answerphone)
e-mail: info@haemophilia-soc.demon.co.uk**
Represents the needs and interests of people with, or affected by, haemophilia.

**Jennifer Trust for Spinal Muscular
Atrophy (SMA)
29B Avon House, New Broad Street
Stratford Upon Avon
Warwickshire CV37 6HW
Tel: 01789 267520
e-mail: anita@jtsma.demon.co.uk
Web site:
http://www.jtsma.demon.co.uk**
For those affected by any form of SMA. Can link families and help to provide equipment.

**MENCAP (Royal Society for
Mentally Handicapped Children
and Adults)
Mencap National Centre
123 Golden Lane, London EC1Y 0RT
Tel: 0171-454 0454**
Provides support and advice for parents of children with mental handicaps.

**Meningitis Research Foundation
133 Gilmore Place
Edinburgh EH3 9PP
Tel: 0131-228 3322
Helpline: 01454 413344 (24 hours)
Web site:
http://www.meningitis.org**

Offers counselling for parents whose children have died from meningitis and gives support to people with loved ones in hospital or at home.

Muscular Dystrophy Group Scottish Council
3rd Floor, Princes House
5 Shandwick Place
Edinburgh EH2 4RG
Tel: 0131-221 0066 (helpline)
e-mail: kengbrown@compuserve.com
Offers practical help and emotional support to sufferers and their families; runs an information and education service for the medical professions, social services and the public.

National Asthma Campaign Scotland
21 Coates Crescent
Edinburgh EH3 7AF
Tel: 0131-226 2544
Asthma helpline: 0345 01 02 03
Web site: http://www.asthma.org.uk
Information and support for people with asthma and their families.

The National Autistic Society Scotland
111 Union Street, Glasgow G1 3TA
Tel: 0141-221 8090
Parent support group which runs an advisory and information service.

National Deaf Children's Society Scotland
100 Norfolk Street, Glasgow G5 9EJ
Tel: 0141-420 3555
Information and advice service on all issues relating to childhood deafness. Offers the expertise of specialist advisors in the fields of education, health, benefits and technology.

National Eczema Society (Scotland)
P.O. Box 2, Arbroath
Angus DD1 4YG
Tel: 01241 853407
Info. line: 0990 11 88 77 (24 hours)
Information, support and advice for people with eczema and their families.

National Meningitis Trust
Fern House, Bath Road
Stroud GL5 3TJ
Tel: 01453 751738
e-mail:
support@meningitis/trust.org.uk
Web site:
http://www.meningitis/trust.org.uk
24-hour helpline: 0345 538118
Free information and support to those suffering from meningitis or who are disabled as a result.

National Society for Phenylketonuria and Allied Disorders
7 Southfield Close
Willen, Milton Keynes MK15 9LL
Helpline: 01908 691653
e-mail: nspku@ukonline.co.uk
Web site:
http://web.ukonline.co.uk/nspku/
Self-help organisation offering information and support to families affected by the disorder.

Reach — Association for Children with Hand or Arm Deficiency
12 Wilson Way, Earls Barton
Northamptonshire NN6 0NZ
Tel: 01604 811041
Scottish branch tel: 01294 272513
Aims to promote the relief of children with upper limb deficiencies by encouraging mutual aid and support between their families.

Research Trust for Metabolic Diseases in Children (RTMDC)
102 Broughton Road
Edinburgh EH7 4JL
Tel: 0131-557 2655
Makes grants and allowances available for the purposes of medical treatment and care of children with metabolic diseases. Puts parents in contact with others in similar circumstances.

Royal National Institute for the Blind (RNIB)
10 Magdala Crescent
Edinburgh EH12 5BE
Tel: 0131-313 1498
Information, services and advice for blind people. **Look Scotland (0131-313 5711)** provides information to parents on services relevant to children with visual impairment.

Scope
12 Park Crescent, London W1N 4EQ
Tel: 0171-636 5020
Helpline: 0800 626 216
e-mail: cphelpline@scope.org.uk
Web site: http://www.scope.org.uk
Provides a range of services for people with cerebral palsy and their families/carers.

Scottish Down's Syndrome Association
158-160 Balgreen Road
Edinburgh EH11 3AU
Tel: 0131-313 4225
Information, advice, counselling and support for parents of children with Down's syndrome.

Scottish Society for Autistic Children
Hilton House, Alloa Business Park
The Whins, Alloa FK10 3SA
Tel: 01259 720044
Provides a range of services in care, support and education for people with autism, their families and carers.

Scottish Spina Bifida Association
190 Queensferry Road
Edinburgh EH4 2BW
Tel: 0131-332 0743
www: http://ourworld.com-puserve.com/homepages/ssbahq
Information, advice, counselling, support and financial help for parents.

SENSE Scotland (National Deaf-Blind and Rubella Association)
5th Floor, Unit 2, 8 Elliot Place
Clydeway Centre, Glasgow G3 8EP
Tel: 0141-221 7577
Textphone: 0141-204 2778
e-mail: kas51@dial.pipex.com
Information, advice and support for families of deaf-blind and rubella handicapped children.

Sickle Cell Society
54 Station Road, Harlesden
London NW10 4UA
Tel: 0181-961 7795/4006
Information, advice and counselling on sickle cell disease and traits.

Society for Mucopolysaccharide Diseases (MPS)
55 Hill Avenue, Amersham
Buckinghamshire HP6 5BX
Tel: 01494 434156
Helpline: 01494 762789
e-mail: 101716.2774@compuserve.com
Web site: http://www.rois.org.uk/mps
Acts as a parent support group; brings about more public awareness of MPS diseases; raises funds for research.

Tay-Sachs Screening Programme
R26 Research Centre
Royal Manchester Children's Hospital
Hospital Road, Pendlebury
Manchester M27 4HA
Tel: 0161-794 4696 ext. 2384 (24 hours)
Screening, information, counselling and practical support to families with present or past history of fatal genetic disorders.

Toxoplasmosis Trust
Room 26, 61-71 Collier Street
London N1 9BE
Helpline: 0171-713 0599
email: info@toxo.org.uk
Information, advice and counselling for pregnant women with toxoplasmosis, parents of infected children and others with toxoplasmosis.

UK Thalassaemia Society
19 The Broadway, Southgate Circus
London N14 6PH
Tel: 0181-882 0011 (helpline)
e-mail: ukts@easynet.co.uk
Education, information, research and counselling offered to sufferers and carriers. Publicity available in many languages.

FAMILY PLANNING

CES (Contraception Education Service)
Helpline: 0171-837 4044

Family Planning Association Scotland
Unit 10 Firrhill Business Centre
76 Firrhill Road, Glasgow G20 7BA
Tel: 0141-576 5088
Aims to promote sexual, emotional and reproductive health, together with planned parenthood, by providing information, publicity, education and training.

Lothian Brook Advisory Centre
2 Lower Gilmore Place
Edinburgh EH3 9NY
Tel: 0131-229 3596
Offers birth control and counselling for younger people on behalf of the NHS. Help and advice on cervical screening; pregnancy testing; abortion referral; counselling for sexual and emotional problems. Free and confidential.

GENERAL SUPPORT

Caesarean Support Network
55 Cooil Drive, Douglas
Isle of Man IM2 2HF
Tel: 01624 661269
Provides support and advice on all matters relating to Caesarean delivery, whether recent or in the past.

Child
Charter House, 43 St Leonards Road
Bexhill-on-Sea, East Sussex TN40 1JA
Tel: 01424 732361 (24 hours)
e-mail: office@email2.child.org.uk
Helps couples coping with problems of infertility and childlessness.

Institute for Complementary Medicine
P.O. Box 194, London SE16 1QZ
Tel: 0171-237 5165
Charity providing information on complementary medicine and referrals to qualified practitioners or helpful organisations.

Life Pregnancy Care
4th Floor, 38 Bath Street
Glasgow G2 1HG
Tel: 0141-332 9656
National hotline: 01926 311511
Campaigns for the repeal of the 1967 Abortion Act. Offers pregnancy and post-abortion counselling, and accommodation for women and their babies.

Marriage Counselling Scotland
105 Hanover Street
Edinburgh EH2 1DJ
Tel: 0131-225 5006
Counselling service for couples with relationship difficulties; irrespective of race, religion, marital status or sexual orientation.

Relate: Marriage Guidance
Herbert Gray College
Little Church Street, Rugby
Warwickshire CV21 3AP
Tel: 01788 573241
Confidential counselling on relationship problems of any kind. Look in the phone book for your local branch under 'Relate' or 'Marriage guidance'.

Samaritans
24-hour emergency line
0345 90 90 90

Scotland Patients' Association
Gartincaber
West Plean
Stirling FK7 8BA
Tel: 01786 818008 (24 hours)
e-mail: scotli@aol.com
Provides advocacy and information to raise awareness of health matters and issues relating to the delivery of services. Deals confidentially with complaints and queries about health services. Can offer medical and legal advice, and an interpreter service.

Shelter Scotland
Head Office
4th Floor
Scotiabank House
South Charlotte Street
Edinburgh EH2 4AW
Tel: 0131-473 7170
Works to relieve poverty and distress among homeless people and campaigns for provision of housing to meet need; runs regional housing aid offices and charity shops.

Women's Health
52 Featherstone Street
London EC1Y 8RT
Tel: 0171-251 6580
e-mail: womenshealth@pop3.pop
tel.co.uk
Information on a wide range of women's health issues. Provides a phone and postal enquiry service, reference library and database to help put women in touch with individuals or groups for self-help and support.

HIV AND AIDS

Body Positive
37-39 Montrose Terrace
Edinburgh EH7 5DJ
Tel: 0131-652 0754
(24 hours)
e-mail: daren@ednet.co.uk
Offers support, advice and counselling to those who are affected by HIV and AIDS, their families, partners and friends.

National AIDS Helpline
Network Scotland
P.O. Box 5000
Glasgow G12 9BL
Helpline: 0800 567 123
(24 Hours)
UK-wide providing free and confidential advice, information and counselling on aspects of HIV, AIDS and sexual health. Produces a wide range of leaflets in many languages. The Helpline can also provide UK-wide referrals to specialist services. All calls are taken by trained and paid staff. Information in other languages: **Welsh** everyday 10am to 2am—0800 371 131. **Bengali** on Tuesdays 6pm to 10pm—0800 371 132. **Gujerati**—0800 371 134; **Urdu**—0800 371 135; **Hindi**—0800 371 136; **Punjabi**—0800 371 133—all on Wednesdays 6pm to 10pm. **Arabic** on Thursdays 6pm to 10pm—0800 282 447. **Cantonese** on Mondays 6pm to 10pm—0800 282 446.

Positively Women
347-349 City Road
London EC1V 1LR
Helpline: 0171-713 0222
Support agency for women living with HIV/AIDS.

LOSS AND BEREAVEMENT

The Compassionate Friends
53 North Street
Bristol BS3 1EN
Helpline: 0117-953 9639
(24 hours)
Nationwide organisation *of* and *for* bereaved parents offering friendship and understanding to other bereaved parents.

Cot Death Helpline
0171-235 1721 (24 hours)

CRUSE Bereavement Care
33-35 Boswall Parkway
Edinburgh EH5 2BR
Tel: 0131-551 1511
Help, support and counselling for bereaved people.

Foundation for the Study of Infant Deaths (Cot Death Research and Support)
14 Halkin Street
London SW1X 7DP
Tel: 0171-235 0965
e-mail: ssid@dial.pipex.com.uk
Personal support and information to parents who have lost a child through cot death. 24-hour helpline. Runs Care of Next Infant (CONI) programme, providing support and advice for families bereaved by cot death with subsequent children.

Scottish Cot Death Trust
Royal Hospital for Sick Children
Yorkhill
Glasgow G3 8SJ
Tel: 0141-357 3946
Support and information for parents bereaved by sudden infant death. Puts parents in touch with local support groups of other bereaved parents.

Stillbirth and Neonatal Death Society (SANDS)
28 Portland Place
London WIN 4DE
Tel: 0171-436 5881 (helpline)
Information and a national network of support groups for bereaved parents.

MENTAL HEALTH

Association for Postnatal Illness (APNI)
25 Jerdan Place
Fulham
London SW6 1BE
Tel: 0171-386 0868
Network of telephone and postal volunteers who have suffered from postnatal illness and offer information, support and encouragement on a one-to-one basis.

Meet A Mum (MAMA)
26 Avenue Road
South Norwood
London SE25 4DX
Tel: 0181-771 5595
Offers information and support to mothers suffering postnatal illness. Helps mothers and mothers-to-be who are isolated and lonely by putting them in touch with others for friendship and support.

Scottish Association for Mental Health (SAMH)
Cumbrae House
15 Carlton Court
Glasgow G5 9JP
Tel: 0141-568 7000
Offers an information service, campaigning and training on mental health issues and deals with any queries on the subject of mental health.

PARENT SUPPORT

BLISSLINK Scotland
19 Victoria Park Gardens South
Glasgow G11 7BX
Tel: 0141-339 9836
(24-hour helpline)
Provides education, resources and support for parents and carers of babies who are, or have been, in special care. Has a listening service, practical advice and support for parents/carers who would like to have a chat.

Cry-sis
BM CRY-SIS
London WC1N 3XX
Tel: 0171-404 5011
Publications: 0161-427 5705
Self-help and support for families with excessively crying, sleepless and demanding children via national helpline. Also by post — please enclose SAE.

Gingerbread Scotland
Community Halls
304 Maryhill Road
Glasgow G20 7YE
Tel: 0141-353 0989/0953
Local groups offer mutual support, friendship, information, advice and practical help to one parent families. Welcomes pregnant women.

Home-Start UK
84 Drymen Road
Glasgow G61 2RH
Tel: 0141-942 3450
Offers friendship, practical help and emotional support to families with under-fives who may be experiencing stress.

National Council for One Parent Families
255 Kentish Town Road
Kentish Town
London NW5 2LX
Tel: 0171-267 1361
Free information for lone parents on welfare rights, benefits, housing, divorce, maintenance, legal rights and bereavement.

One Parent Families Scotland
13 Gayfield Square
Edinburgh EH1 3NX
Tel: 0131-556 3899/4563
e-mail: opfs@gn.apc.org
Web site: http://www.gn.apc.org/opfs
Helps pregnant women, parents bringing up children alone and non-custodial parents. Offers information on welfare rights, housing, childcare, sources of financial help, education and self-help groups.

One Plus — One Parent Families
55 Renfrew Street, Glasgow G2 3BD
Tel: 0141-333 1450
Independent organisation for one parent families offering information, advice and counselling for individuals and groups of lone parents and their children. Campaigns to achieve equality of opportunities for lone parents whether single, widowed, divorced or separated and regardless of sex, sexuality, race, colour or religion. Managed by lone parents themselves.

Twins and Multiple Births Association (TAMBA)
22 Mansewood Road
Glasgow G43 1TN
Tel: 0141-632 4470
TAMBA Twinline: 01732 868000
Web site: http://www.surreycc.gov.uk/tamba
Scottish branch of TAMBA. Coordinates network of twins clubs across Scotland, offering support to parents. Contact for details of local clubs.

PREGNANCY AND MATERNITY SERVICES

AIMS (Association for Improvements in the Maternity Services)
40 Leamington Terrace
Edinburgh EH10 4JL
Tel: 0131-229 6259 (helpline)
Voluntary pressure group offering support and advice about parents' rights, complaints procedures and choices within maternity care, including home birth.

Lothian Homebirth Support Group
87 Joppa Road, Edinburgh EH15
Tel: 0131-669 1971
Provides support and advice for women trying to arrange a homebirth. Telephone for help and advice.

Maternity Alliance
45 Beech Street, London EC2P 2LX
Tel: 0171-588 8583
Helpline: 0171-588 8582
e-mail: ma@mail.pro-net.co.uk
Campaigns for improvements in rights and services for mothers, fathers and babies. Provides advice on health care, benefits and employment rights and an information service for parents and professionals.

The National Childbirth Trust
Alexandra House
Oldham Terrace,
Acton, London W3 6NH
Tel: 0181-992 8637
Offers antenatal classes and postnatal support.

Scottish Birth Teachers Association (SBTA)
40 Leamington Terrace
Edinburgh EH10 4JL
Tel: 0131-229 6259
Offers antenatal and postnatal classes.

Scottish Independent Midwives
1 Morning Hill
Peebles EH45 9JS
Tel: 01721 729601
Support group offering help, information and support to women wanting home birth and maternity care information. Antenatal, postnatal and aquanatal classes.

PREGNANCY PROBLEMS

Action on Pre-eclampsia (APEC)
31-33 College Road
Harrow, Middlesex HA1 1EJ
Tel: 0181-863 3271
Helpline: 01923 266778
Charity providing support and research for sufferers of pre-eclampsia.

Association of Chartered Physiotherapists in Women's Health ACPWH c/o Chartered Society of Physiotherapy
14 Bedford Row
London WC1R 4ED
Support and information for women with dysfunctional symphisis pubis and other problems related to pregnancy and birth which would benefit from physiotherapy.

Dysfunctional Symphisis Pubis (DSP) British DSP Support Group
17 Muir Road, Dumpton
Ramsgate, Kent CT11 8AX
Support and information for women with DSP.

Miscarriage Association
15 Clerwood Bank
Edinburgh EH12 8PZ
Tel: 0131-334 8883 (helpline)
Information, advice and support for women who have had, or who are having, a miscarriage.

Obstetric Cholestasis Support Group
4 Shenstone Close
Sutton, Coldfield B74 4XB
Tel: 0121-353 0699
Support and information.

Support Around Termination for Abnormality (SATFA)
73-75 Charlotte Street
London W1P 1LB
Helpline: 0171-631 0285
Offers support and information to women and couples who have had a diagnosis of abnormality in their unborn baby, and provides continued support to those parents who have a termination of pregnancy.

RIGHTS AND BENEFITS

ACAS (Advisory, Conciliation and Arbitration Service)
Franborough House
123-157 Bothwell Street
Glasgow G2 7JR
Tel: 0141-248 1400
Public enquiry service: 0141-204 2677
Provides advice on time off for antenatal care and on matters such as unfair dismissal. For your nearest contact, look in the phone book or ask at your local library or Citizen's Advice Bureau.

Benefit Enquiry Line
0800 88 22 00
Textphone: 0800 24 33 55
Confidential telephone advice and information service, for people with disabilities, their carers and representatives. Offers general advice and information about social security benefits and how to claim them.

Child Support Agency
P.O. Box 55, Pedmore House
Brierley Hill, West Midlands DY5 1YL
Enquiry line: 0345 133133
Government agency which assesses and collects child maintenance in Great Britain. Advice about child benefit, one parent benefit and guardian's allowance.

Citizens' Advice Bureaux (CABs)
Ask at your local library or look in your phone book under 'Counselling and Advice'.

Commission for Racial Equality
45 Hanover Street, Edinburgh
EH2 2PJ
Tel: 0131-226 5186
e-mail: info@cre.gov.uk
Web site: www.open.gov.uk/cre/crehome.htm
Works for the elimination of unlawful racial discrimination and the promotion of equal opportunities and good race relations.

Edinburgh Disability Benefits Centre
Argyle House, 3 Lady Lawson Street
Edinburgh EH3 0XY
Tel: 0131-229 9191
Helpline: 0345 123 456
Information and advice on Attendance Allowance and Disability Living Allowance. Deals with all areas in Scotland except Strathclyde (see Glasgow DBC).

Equal Opportunities Commission
Stock Exchange House
7 Nelson Mandela Place
Glasgow G2 1QW
Tel: 0141-248 5833
Information and advice on issues of discrimination and equal opportunities.

Family Credit Helpline
01253 50 00 50

Glasgow Disability Benefits Centre
Corunna House, 29 Cadogan Street
Glasgow G2 7BN
Tel: 0141-249 3500
Information and advice on Attendance Allowance and Disability Living Allowance. Covers Strathclyde.

Social Security, Department of
For general advice on all social security benefits, child support, pensions and National Insurance, including maternity benefits and income support. Telephone, write or call into your local social security office.

Social Services and Welfare Organisations
For information on topics including benefits, housing, financial difficulties, employment, relationship problems, childcare and useful organisations. Look up 'Social Services' in the phone book under the name of your local authority or ask at your local library.

VEGETARIANISM

Vegetarian Society of the UK Ltd
Parkdale, Dunham Road, Altringham
Cheshire WA14 4QG
Tel: 0161-928 0793
e-mail: bron@vegsoc.demon.co.uk
For general information and advice on all aspects of vegetarianism. Produces a wide range of resources including booklets on vegetarianism for babies, children and pregnant women.

Index